NO TIME
TO KISS GOODBYE

WARTIME CHILDREN FLEEING
TO THE COUNTRYSIDE

by
Harry Clement

This book is dedicated to Ray Lamb, an ex-evacuee, who died in January 1995.
Ray was an enthusiast for this book, who reasoned that these stories should be told in
order that future generations might know how children can be involved in war.

To Patsy, my wife, God bless you for your untiring support.

First published in Great Britain
by Harry Clement June 1995

ISBN No.   0 9525924 0 1

Printed in England
Produced by Print Matters, Harlow. 01279 302095

CONTENTS

PREFACE

The schoolroom was crowded with people, their voices raised to the level of a swarm of bees in June. There was much kissing, hugging and shaking of hands. Tears were being shed and comments such as, "It's nearly fifty years since I last saw you" or "You know, you haven't changed a bit, I would have known you anywhere." The last comment being somewhat incongruous, seeing that the last time the speaker had seen the subject of such misconception, was when they were children together. At gatherings such as these, illogical or flattering terms were accepted.

The schoolmaster, video-camera in hand, would occasionally push his way through the dense throng, halt in the rare isolation that a few score inches of bare floor boards would give him, and then fire off a few more dozen frames of film, to record for posterity, this gathering of middle-aged men and women, whose accents denounced them as not being 'locals'.

Reaching the far end of the room, the schoolmaster turned, filmed the scene, and then lowering the camera, gazed with awe at this noisy group. He wished for a moment that he had instead, the usual morning-assembly bunch of schoolchildren. Fleetingly, a pained expression crossed his face, to be instantly removed by a beaming smile as someone turned and gave him a nod. Raising the camera again, he made some more records of historical importance.

The date was the 13th October 1990 and the collection of people had arrived at the village school in Clovelly, North Devon, for a week-end of re-union with their past, 1940 to be exact. Most of these middle-aged men and women had first come to Clovelly in June 1940, evacuees from the threat of Hitler's bombers, that delighted in raining terror on innocent civilians. They had returned in answer to a nationwide radio announcement that a re-union was planned if there was sufficient interest. This was now evident from the crowd that had arrived, even from Nevada in the USA.

Following this initial meeting and the consumption of much tea,coffee and cakes, served by schoolchildren and their parents, the newcomers adjourned to the local hostelry or village homes, for lunch.

Their next gathering was at 6-30pm in the little parish church where over 250 people packed the pews and there was standing room only for the latecomers. A service of thanksgiving was held, with the lessons read by two of the ex-evacuees and the address given by myself.

Repeating the words of the address within these pages, serves to describe once again the depth of gratitude felt by the ex-evacuees towards the old families of Clovelly and to their erstwhile schoolfriends.

" It is more than appropriate that our Thanksgiving Service is being held in Clovelly Parish Church. This building is steeped in history with the earliest recorded patron of this church being Queen Matilda, wife of William the Conqueror.

The wars and battles of yesteryear did not involve the mass evacuation of children and vulnerable citizens, and from those early wars fought on or around our coasts, the wars moved abroad, inflicting death and hardship on soldier, sailor and citizen alike.

If we cast our minds back to our history books, to recall such names as Trafalgar, Waterloo, the Imperial territory seeking wars of the Victoria period, the Great War of 1914 - 18 (which was the war to end all wars), until we come to the conflict of 1939 - 45.

It was a brilliant idea of the government, no doubt born out of desperation, to evacuate all children of school age to those areas considered safe from aerial attack. This was varied to include younger children, if there was someone to look after them. Some of the places originally chosen, were themselves bombed, so the children were moved again.

The first school party of evacuees to arrive in Clovelly, came from two areas of London - Deptford and Peckham. The two schools had not met one another until 14 June 1940, when we made that train journey from London to Bideford. At Exeter Central Railway Station, ladies in white aprons busied themselves serving we excited children from tables loaded with cake, tarts and sandwiches. At Bideford, the hospitality was repeated, but with the addition of a scrubbing before we ate. I think the idea was to feed us to stop us talking, as they did not understand us anyway, nor in those early days, did we understand them. We soon came to know that feeding well your guest was a Devon tradition.

Later, we were followed in February and May of 1941, by children escaping the bombing of Bristol and Plymouth, and they too, became our friends. Some are present this evening.

We came as refugees from the horrors of war to the quiet tranquillity of Clovelly. You people of Clovelly took us in, you fed us and you looked after our welfare. We grew to love you - and many of us adopted your way of life and dialect, so much so, that in many instances, our parents could not understand some of the things we said, especially " Wer begwain " and " The maister zayz zo."

The children returned back to their city homes at various stages, some within a few months, where family circumstances were such that mum wanted the family around her; others went back when the blitz had ended, and others when the war in Europe had come to an end. One remained until 1947 and another remained, later married and is still here.

We learnt from you something of the richness of Devon and we hope that we have left some pleasant memories behind with you.

Fifty years after we first came to Clovelly, this re-union is a pilgrimage, made, in order to thank the more senior members of the congregation, with the sons, daughters and grand-children of those who opened their homes to us, and to those erstwhile school friends who shared their school with us, to you all, who opened your hearts to accept us into your midst, in those war-torn and troubled times of the early 1940's, we who have returned, say a grateful and sincere thank you."

A wall plaque, expressing the gratitude of the ex-evacuees, was presented to the people of Clovelly. Many, who had been unable to arrive in time for the school tea party, were now greeting long forgotten school friends, both evacuees and local.

The dinner that followed, for over 200 people, was held in the parish hall and like similar functions was in an atmosphere of excited happiness. Much food and drink was consumed by the evacuees and their local guests; records and tapes of music from war-time Britain was relayed throughout the evening. Dancing went on into the early hours.

Like holiday friendships, vows were made to 'never lose touch with one another ever again'.

This book is the story of the memories that some of these middle-aged men and women still have from those far distant days, when as frightened or excited, but nevertheless homesick children, they left their parents in the cities to come to the peaceful haven of Clovelly. Each chapter is a story, the reminiscences of those well past their two score years and ten. Some instances of recall were prompted by a related story or another version of the same incident seen from a different pair of eyes. Each story is a mixture of a child's excitement and sadness in those terrible years of the early 1940's.

Sadly, not everyone answered the appeal to relate their memories. With some it is understood, for it would be ridiculous to expect that every child found a friendly and welcome home in Clovelly. The law of averages would perhaps dictate that there would be a few homes where the child would be made to feel miserable, where there was a lack of human love or understanding. In other instances, occupiers of houses invited members of their families to come and stay with them, so obviating the possibility of having to take in evacuees once the house was full.

Gratefully, these instances were so few as to make them outstanding and the individual householders marked by their peers who, shunned them and commented variously, "They'm no good you know, they were terrible to that poor little maid. They made her life a misery before she was moved from them."

To the large majority of evacuees, both from London and Bristol, Clovelly was a place of love and friendship. A place to run, to roam, to wander, to stay and pause awhile, to take in the beautiful scenery and share the friendship of the majority of the local people.

It was a new life, something they had never seen before, no running water in the homes, toilet (earth or bucket) at the bottom of the garden and no electricity or gas. More animals than they had ever seen in their lives before, many of which they had only seen either in books or on the cinema screen. The paraffin oil lamps to light the homes was something to gaze at, it appeared every home had a different make, shape or colour, as they gave their warm and comforting golden glow across the room. The Methodist Chapel had oil lamps hanging from the ceiling which were pulled down on pulleys in order to light them or adjust the wicks. Firewood played a bigger part in everyone's lives, for it was essential, not only to warm the home, but in many instances to cook with.

So it was that they returned to Clovelly to relive those childhood days and memories, to meet old friends, and to visit places in the village, cliff-tops and woods, of which, time had merely frayed the clarity in their memory.

It is hoped that this collection of stories will serve as a memorial to those elderly Clovelly folk still living in the area, and to the memory of those who have passed on, who took us in and loved us, in those war torn years of the early 1940's. Although their devotion is an example to all who believe in human charity, we should pray that children will never again be forced to be uprooted from their homes in time of war, or parents be faced with the dilemma of choosing whether to send their children to a unknown destination of possible safety, or have them remain with them to face probable death.

CHAPTER ONE
WHY THE CHILDREN HAD TO GO

In March 1939, Hitler ordered his troops into Czechoslovakia, and it was obvious to many British people, that notwithstanding Chamberlain's attempts to appease Hitler and thereby secure 'peace in our time'; there would be war with Germany and it would not be long in coming. What many saw and Chamberlain failed to recognise, was that you cannot expect to feed a ferocious and rabid beast with titbits and expect that will suffice. If the titbits are willingly given or no resistance shown to the beast's demands, then regardless of any agreement, these claims will be taken by force if necessary.

Germany faced an alliance of at least two weak governments in Britain and France, both of whom were acutely aware of the grotesque losses sustained in the Great War of 1914-18, and Germany knew that they would go to enormous lengths to avoid war with Germany again. Britain's lack of 'stomach' for fighting a war had been demonstrated in 1936 when they had failed to intervene in Italy's inhumane aggression in Ethiopia.

In 1937, Germany's assistance to Franco in the Spanish Civil War and the testing of his Luftwaffe power with the terror bombing of Guernica by the German Condor Squadron, received nothing more than mild reprimands from our political leaders. Who can wonder then that Hitler and his advisers saw Britain's reluctance to get involved, as a weakness, and as such, need not be feared as a future adversary likely to oppose the demands that Germany were about to make on the world.

Neville Chamberlain might have gained the impression that Hitler was a gentleman, "...who could be relied upon to keep his word", but many British politicians outside of the government did not share his views. The appeasers had for some time regarded Winston Churchill as a 'warmonger' and warned that his rantings should be disregarded. Churchill's speeches in the House of Commons and elsewhere, and his writings also, continually espoused dire warnings if Britain did not take heed of this threat of a re-armed Germany. Britain's defences, he thundered, required a massive upgrading and modernising to bring it anywhere near a proper force to be reckoned with. He demanded that plans be put into effect at once to build new and more powerful warships, aircraft and tanks. However, Churchill was a prophet calling in the wilderness.

That Germany in March 1939, should then trundle forward the blatantly obvious excuses and propaganda over Danzig, and cast hints at what it might do to Poland if its claims were not met, was hardly surprising; after all, they did not expect that Britain and France were going to do anything about it, they would be sitting on their hands on the side-lines like chastened children, watching but doing nothing.

However, Mr Chamberlain did announce to the House on 31 March 1939 that if Poland felt its independence threatened and forced to resist any threat by force, Britain would come to Poland's support.

Irrespective of Neville Chamberlain's opinion of Hitler, the British public had no liking of the man or his cronies. Listeners in pubs, clubs and homes throughout the land would have discovered that public opinion were displaying that long established trait of the British, they hated bullies and they always championed the underdog. The general agreement was that "...someone ought to smack him one before he gets too big for himself." If Chamberlain did not hear this, then he was out of touch with the British people.

The Danzig excuse boiled over into violence with lives being lost on the border between Germany and Poland. Germany, putting on a false air of injured pride and patient diplomacy, demanded that its claims be met. No doubt remembering the earlier help Chamberlain had given him in forcing President Benes of Czechoslovakia to acede to Germany's demands for territory, Hitler hoped that once again Britain might persuade an awkward neighbour to give up part of their land to Germany.

On 1 September 1939, Germany invaded Poland with men and tanks, whilst the Luftwaffe bombed defenceless towns and cities in a repetition of Guernica, demonstrating to the world that anyone, or any place, would be a target for his new found terror machine – the Luftwaffe.

The following day, there was a revolt in the House of Commons, when members from both sides of the House demanded firm and positive action from Chamberlain. They were suspicious that another 'Munich' was under preparation and by ten-thirty that evening the cabinet had joined them. Chamberlain was absent from the chamber by this time and when the members discovered where Chamberlain was dining, they descended en masse to his table. As if to illustrate the mood of the MP.'s and the feeling of the nation, the brief meeting at the table was accompanied by tremendous claps of thunder.

Chamberlain bowed to the members' demands and instructed the British Ambassador in Berlin to deliver an ultimatum to Hitler at nine o'clock the following morning, the 3 September. That unless Britain received satisfactory assurance by 11 am that Germany had stopped all aggressive action against Poland and start to withdraw from captured territory, a state of war would exist."

It is said that after the ultimatum was delivered to the German Foreign Ministry and Hitler was aware of its contents, he angrily called out to his advisers, "What now" and Goering remarked to Hitler, "If we lose this war, may heaven be merciful to us."

At quarter past eleven on Sunday 3 September, the Prime Minister, Neville Chamberlain spoke to the nation. Other than those who were already in their churches, most of the nation had switched on their radios at about ten o'clock, waiting for some news of Germany's response to the ultimatum, when Chamberlain spoke it was obvious straight away that it was to be war.

The Prime Minister announced that as no such undertaking had been received, this nation was at war with Germany. France followed the British example and as from five o'clock that afternoon, she too was at war with Germany.

That evening, the King spoke to the nation and the Commonwealth. He concluded his speech by saying, "The task will be hard. There may be dark days ahead and war can no longer be confined to the battlefield, but we can only do the right as we see the right and reverently commit our cause to God. If one and all we keep resolutely faithful to it, ready for whatever service or sacrifice it may demand, then, with God's help we shall prevail. May He bless and keep us all."

As soon as the news was known throughout the world, Britain's family, the Commonwealth, came to her assistance when Australia and New Zealand declared war on Germany. Canada followed on the 6 September.

Straight away a War Cabinet was formed and Churchill was brought in from the wilderness to be First Lord of the Admiralty. This announcement brought great joy to many, especially the Royal Navy, when a special message was sent around the fleets to announce, "Winston's back."

It was announced that petrol rationing was to begin on 16 September and that only one grade of petrol would be sold, at one shilling and sixpence a gallon. The compulsory call-up for war service of men from the age of 21 years to 40 was to begin, those aged between 18 and 20 would not be called-up except in the last emergency.

Items in the newspapers included advertisements for tobacco at elevenpence halfpenny an ounce, cigarettes at one shilling and twopence for twenty, brandy at seventeen shillings a bottle and a rash of articles that would now be needed in the home – blackout material, iodine and heaters for the shelters.

Gas-masks had already been issued to millions of people, a standard one for adults and children down to about five years; a 'Mickey Mouse' type for small children, with a red exhaling valve on the front, like a nose; and a special one for toddlers and babies that was all enclosing with a clear see through panel at the top and a hand pump at the side.

For the first time, people were seeing policemen wearing steel helmets with the word POLICE written in white paint across the front, and the 'bobby' wore his military style gas-mask slung over his shoulder as he patrolled the streets. As the helmets weighed nearly three pounds, their adoption by the police was not a popular one nor willingly taken. Steel helmets were now being worn by members of the London Fire Brigade as well as the newly created Air-raid Wardens, whose only indication of what they did was an arm-band worn over their ordinary clothes.

It was then announced that registration of all males between the ages of 18 – 41 was to take place, but that men would be called up in age groups, one year age difference every day, i.e. 28 year olds on Wednesday, 29 year olds on Thursday.

Notices were displayed everywhere as well as in the newspapers giving details of what time the groups should register, usually the A – C's would be the first of the day at eight-thirty in the morning.

A black-out was enforced in all homes as well as in shops, industry and motor vehicles. Special vehicle headlamp visors could be bought, which gave only a thin horizontal slit of light, which although not giving sufficient illumination to drive at more than a very modest speed, allowed stumbling pedestrians and other road users to see them. The black-out was vigorously enforced by air-raid wardens and uniform police officers and in these early days of the war, a succession of warnings would be heard just after dark every day, and would usually take the form of, "Put that light out ." This normally meant that there was a chink of light shining around a poorly fitted curtain, or that a door had been opened to throw a beam of light outside the house.

Rumours abounded, which although very widely dispersed, were not discounted by the authorities, perhaps even encouraged, that an airman at several thousand feet was able to see a cigarette glowing in the lips of the smoker on the ground. No wonder the police and air-raid wardens carried out their duties with so much fervour.

Theatres, cinemas and other places of public entertainment were ordered to be closed until further notice; but this restriction was to be lifted after a short while.

One newspaper columnist wrote in his paper on the 4 September that he had passed by Buckingham Palace the previous day and had seen the Changing of the Guard. "drab khaki-suited guardsmen were brought to the palace in lorries and although they would probably prove to be effective, they did not display the splendour and excitement they always did when dressed in scarlets.'

The newspapers carried a rash of items from their catering correspondents, under the heading of 'Wartime Recipes' and householders were urged not to stockpile food, but at the same time, the newspapers carried items, urging everyone to make sure that their garden air-raid shelter held a stock of essential things, such as candles, paraffin for the heater, first-aid equipment and some tinned food.

Some children had already been evacuated prior to the announcement of war, but as 1939 moved into 1940, with British troops already in position in France, the atmosphere of impending peril in the form of bombing attacks on our cities, gradually intensified and further plans for the evacuation of the cities and what was considered to be 'areas at risk', i.e. invasion danger spots.

The responsibility of organising this was shared by the Ministry's of Education and Health, and it was stated in the House of Commons that out of a school population of 500,000 children, only some 120,000 were to be evacuated according to their parents wishes.

Suggestions were made in the House of Commons that the evacuation be made compulsory, but the government could only see immense problems if that were to be announced. Many parents stated that they would refuse to comply with compulsory evacuation or indeed any form of separation from their children. Many parents saying that the family must stick together, "We are all going to die together."

The pace of war speeded up in April 1940, when Germany invaded Denmark and Norway, and British and Allied forces were sent to Norway in an attempt to drive them out. Within two months, German forces had occupied all of Norway.

In such times of peril, the feeling of the Members in the House of Commons were such that they despaired of Mr Chamberlain and his leadership of the government. Mr Leo Emery,, a long time friend of Churchill, rose to his feet in the Chamber and directing himself to the Prime Minister, dramatically repeated the words of Oliver Cromwell, "You have sat too long here for any good you are doing. Depart, I say, and let us have done with you. In the name of God, go."

So Neville Chamberlain resigned as leader of the government and Churchill succeeded him on 10 May 1940, to form a National Government.

Soon after, he made the first of a succession of famous wartime speeches. It included his immortal words, "I have nothing to offer, but blood, toil, tears and sweat."

On 15 May, the government announced the formation of the Local Defence Force, the L.D.V., the forerunner of the Home Guard.

May saw the invasion of Holland and Belgium by the Germans, followed by their forces driving into France. Heavily engaged but outnumbered by men, guns, tanks and aircraft, the Allies withdrew to the beaches of Dunkirk, where, beginning on the 27 May and continuing non-stop, until 4 June, the evacuation of 65% of the British Expeditionary Force was completed. The successful evacuation of not only 225,000 British troops and service personnel, but many thousand French troops as well.

Operation Dynamo, as it was named, was carried out in the face of the most fearful aerial bombardment, that cost countless lives, ships and equipment. The RAF lost 106 aircraft, the Luftwaffe between 130 – 140 aircraft. 243 Allied ships had been sunk (out of 1000 in the operation) and of these 6 were British destroyers, the French losing 7 destroyers.

There were hundreds of acts of heroism, with many more stories depicting them and the experiences of those taking part. One story that says much for the close bonds that existed between the rescuers and those waiting for salvation, which is related by Christopher Hibbert in his writing of Operation Dynamo is where the peace-time pleasure steamer Medway Queen is hove to,just off the beach at Dunkirk, waiting to take men on board. Mr Brett from the steamer wades ashore, calling out, "I want sixty men." There was no reply. He reached a causeway where a line of waiting troops, all queued in an orderly column. A sergeant stepped up, "Sixty men, yes sir" and calmly detailed the appropriate number to follow Mr Brett. The sergeant placed one man's hand in Mr Brett's. The man had been blinded and when he was told he was being taken to safety, he replied simply and politely, "Thanks mate "and allowed himself to be led out into deeper water to the waiting boats.

On Sunday 2 June, Churchill was in his office, dictating another speech, his report to the House on the evacuation from Dunkirk. According to his secretary, Mary Shearburn, he began, "We must be very careful not to assign to this deliverance, the attributes of a victory…" He continued dictating, there were long pauses, then he would utter some more lines as he paced up and down the room. Midnight came and went, Miss Shearburn grew tired, Churchill's voice grew fainter, his head was bowed, he was fighting tears as he went on. As sobs in his dictation made the words hard to hear, he said, "We shall not flag or fail. We shall go on to the end. We shall fight in France, we shall fight in the seas and the oceans, we shall defend our island whatever the cost may be. We shall fight on the beaches, we shall fight on the landing grounds, we shall fight in the fields and in the streets, we shall fight in the hills…" Emotionally drained, Churchill could not go on, but then he recovered himself, "We shall NEVER surrender."

After he had got through that part, Miss Shearburn recollects that the tears had left his voice. He went on, "Even if, which I do not for a moment believe, this island or a large part of it were subjugated and starving, then our empire beyond the seas would carry on the struggle…" His final phrase was dictated at a faster tempo as he thundered, "…until, in God's good time, the New World, with all its power and might, steps forth to the rescue and liberation of the Old."

On 14 June the newspapers announced with banner headlines, "All church bells silenced from today. L.D.V.'s will toll warning in invasion."

Another item in the newspapers was the report that several Young Fascists had been arrested, charged and convicted of sabotage. All these case arose from acts where they had damaged or wrecked machinery being used in war work. Another man, an ardent Communist, was also convicted for a similar offence.

But this was also a very important day for a number of school children in London; this was the day they were to leave their homes and families and take part in a great adventure as they set off in one of the parties of the mass evacuation programme.

The march through the streets from their schools to the station was watched and followed, not only by anxious mothers, but by plenty of onlookers as well. For most Londoners, the war had altered everything, sandbags around some of the buildings, the parks dug up with trenches and air-raid shelters, barrage balloons flying over London, seemingly with every green space occupied by the windlass trucks that controlled the balloons and with everyone carrying their gasmasks wherever they went, it appeared that the world had gone mad.

The children were saying goodbye to all this, to the army crews that manned the anti-aircraft guns in the parks, to the airmen who manned the balloon windlass trucks and to the many other sights that showed that London was at war.

Every school had one or two teachers that were being evacuated with the children and the authorities also send a sufficient number of adult escorts to try to control and shepherd the children. Although buses were used a great deal, it was the trains that carried the bulk of the children to the country in those two to three weeks following Dunkirk.

The government had issued decrees in the form of Emergency Powers, that gave authority to local councils in the reception areas to act as evacuation officers with the responsibility to house the children. Those people who did not volunteer to take in children and whom the local evacuation officers thought should, had compulsory billeting orders served upon them. Although this enabled many children to have roofs over their heads, it did not provide them with a home; such reluctance to help and lack of Christian spirit, inevitably led to many problems which usually, to save any more problems, led to the householder getting their way and the children being removed. When this became general knowledge in the area, it brought scorn and anger from their more kindly disposed neighbours. Even after the war it would occasionally be remarked, "Do you remember her, miserable devil wouldn't take in any evacuees, said that she wasn't well enough. She's alright now though, filling her place up with visitors 'cause they pay more."

A correspondent, writing of Bideford in the 'Bideford and North Devon Gazette', stated that, "I was surprised to see and hear of the numbers of those who had been explaining that they could not see their way to complying with the orders. Just occasionally, in the talking groups, I heard expressions of opinion of which the speakers ought to have been ashamed." He went on to say that there was a goodness of heart which far outweighed any other feeling, after all, youngsters could not help coming to the area. Bideford is the nearest town to Clovelly, only ten miles, and what was written about Bideford, might not have applied to Clovelly. Certainly no reports of any compulsory orders were heard of and no research since has unearthed any evidence. I know of one case where a little girl aged five years, was billeted in a home where the foster parents had their own children of similar age. The little evacuee was packed off to bed whilst the householders children was allowed to stay up and play or listen to the radio. On one occasion, the eldest girl took the little evacuee to visit some people who lived in a farm across the fields and as they had been warned not to be late back for the evening meal, the evacuee was worried about the length of time that they stayed at the farm. When they returned home, the foster mother was waiting at the door and berated the little evacuee girl for being late, gave her a thrashing and sent her to bed without any food. Her own daughter was not touched and stayed downstairs to have her meal. Such cruelty was not widely known at the time, but now those children are adults they are speaking out, although, in general, the perpetrators are now dead.

Certainly the local authorities made the evacuees very welcome when they arrived at Bideford Railway Station, even though they had been told to expect something like 4000 evacuees in one week. The Mayor, together with the Chairman of the District Council, and crowds of local people came to meet the train that arrived from London on the 14 June 1940. Organised into groups of helpers to carry the belongings of the London children, were the local Boy Scouts, Girl Guides, Sea Cadets, Sea Scouts, Church Lads Brigade and many others. For the toddlers and those who were sick, there were cars and buses. Eventually, this train load were distributed to the various halls and schools in Bideford, where washing facilities and food had been arranged for them. Buses were then waiting to take the children to Clovelly and the other areas nominated to receive them.

Alas, the brilliant organisation to evacuate the children to rural areas was not matched by any arrangements to have them integrated into the local schools.

The mass evacuation programme of school children might have been on the desks of Whitehall civil servants for many months prior to them being put into effect, but although the various county education authorities were aware that there would probably be some sort of evacuation to rural areas, the timing and scale that the children left the cities, London in particular, apparently caught them off balance as far as the schools were concerned. Even if they would have protested at the time, that 'everything had gone to plan', it is obvious from old correspondence, that they did not pass on the early warning to village school heads.

In Clovelly, the sudden influx of so many children from Peckham and Deptford in South London, nearly brought the village school to a halt. From a register of under thirty pupils, the school head was now faced to accommodate an increase of another 160 plus, children from London.

It was obvious to anyone that the building and set-up of classes could not hold the children in its present form. A rapid re-think had to be done by Mr Hesketh, the Head teacher but in the meantime, there simply was no room for the new arrivals. They had come down to Clovelly with some of their own teachers and after some discussion with them, Mr Hesketh decided that whilst the weather was fine, the older newcomers could separate into classes and be taught by their own teachers outside in the countryside.

This involved walking the lanes and woods for nature study, pausing frequently to do mental arithmetic and take part in 'spelling bees'. It is true to say that many children had not had a proper sit-down lesson for nearly a year.

As far as Bellenden Road School in Peckham was concerned, classes had more or less ceased to exist from just after the outbreak of war. The school had closed down for quite a lengthy period and when it did re-open, there were so few teachers that children aged from five to eleven were all grouped together in one class. This was in the days when small infant children used to sleep for an hour every afternoon and small folding beds were provided in the London schools for this purpose. With the war time grouping at Bellenden Road School, there was the indignity for the older children of being forced to lie down on the little beds as their younger colleagues were used to doing. Arriving in Clovelly in the following June, they were faced once again with the prospect of having no proper classes. Because of no proper preparation for their arrival and the consequent effect they would have on a small village school, they were condemned, although this probably would not be the word chosen by the children, to wait another three months before they could enter a school and sit or stand to take lessons in a classroom again.

This was at a time when most city children were constantly hoping that during the night German bombs would hit their empty school. The sound of 'Yippee' would echo around the streets.

It says much for the ability, devotion and ingenuity of the teachers at this time, that this missed period in the children's schooling did not result in the complete failure of the children's education. Irrespective of the chaos, the teachers did more than what could properly be expected from them, and attempted to school their charges in the three 'Rs', as if in a perfect setting. That they succeeded was due more to their calling and expertise than the facilities provided by higher authority.

Even before the London evacuees had been found room in the school, German bombers had raided London; when in a night attack on the 24 August they hit the centre of the city, although the mass raids did not take place until 7 September.

It would not be until 20 September 1940 that the Education Authorities met Mr Hesketh, to agree with him that all three schools (Clovelly, Deptford and Peckham) be merged into one school under Mr Hesketh. Swift to act, he merged the school on the 23 September. The Education Authority leased the old St. Peter's chapel, down in the village of Clovelly, as an overspill classroom for the infants.

This solved some of the overcrowding in the school but it also presented problems to some of the children, where an older child had a younger brother or sister to look after. That meant leaving for school early, passing by the school and walking down the steep lane under the trees that lead to the top of the cobbled street of Clovelly. Situated in a back street half-way down the village was the little chapel and the older child would have to leave their charge for the day. It also involved leaving school the moment classes finished in the afternoon and run all the way down again to meet the younger one.

Because of the overcrowding and lack of desks, there had to be some friction between the children, but Mr Hesketh's method of discipline was equal to the occasion. Dispensing punishment in the form of the cane, which the Londoners were well used to, he maintained order in what had all the ingredients of bedlam and anarchy. An organised Christmas Carol Concert finally cemented relations between everyone.

Hardly had Mr Hesketh got matters straightened out with his overgrown school when in February 1941, forty children and one teacher arrived from Bristol. After a while these were also absorbed and things were more organised again. Some of the London children had returned home for various reasons, attitudes of their Clovelly foster parents, the child's failure to adapt to country life, the incompatibility of the child/foster parent relationship or sadly, very often a fatality at the family home during a raid. Often, it was found among the younger children, that the trauma of being separated from their parents and all that they held dear, had brought on a spate of bed-wetting, which occasionally resulted in the child being sent back to London.

In May 1941, a further surge in numbers came when fifty odd children and a teacher arrived from Plymouth. This was a very mixed group of so many different ages and they were all billeted in the New Inn Hotel, half-way down the cobbled High Street of Clovelly village. Somehow, Mr Hesketh and his staff fitted them all in.

In order that the evacuees did not put too much of a strain on the food rations of the fosterparents, the Education Authority leased the old former coach-house of the Rectory as a canteen. This, and the accompanying buildings were converted into a form of kitchen and dining room and in May 1941, it opened for business.

The older boys were already engaged in managing a garden not far from the school and the produce went to the canteen. A new plot was offered rent free by Clovelly Estate and this, 'Wonnacott's', was taken in hand by the boys and Mr Hesketh, who always worked alongside his pupils. Soon the wilderness of brambles, weeds and tall grass was dug and after much sweat and back ache, was producing salads and vegetables for the canteen. It is recorded that in the first term of its operation, the canteen served over 7000 dinners to the children.

In the school holiday time, the children, particularly those who were living in Higher Clovelly, worked on the farms at hay and corn harvesting and potato picking. As it was all so alien to them, they surprised the farmers as to how much they enjoyed the work, which was often repetitive. These children were the ones who liked the countryside and its way of life, also it would be these children that later sorely missed the fresh air and open spaces that Clovelly had afforded them.

The reports that Mr Hesketh sent to the Education Authority, showed how much he was indebted to his staff, singling out Miss Place and Mr Bamsey for special mention. He often complained of the form filling that he was obliged to do and in one report stated, "our work is multiplied beyond measure by the deluge of forms, statistical returns and clothing sheets which we are required to furnish to various authorities."

In another report he wrote, "This war has found many victims besides those who have perished in battle and bombing raids. One of these has been education which has suffered severely. Constant evacuations and staff changes, extraneous tasks presented to schools by the various authorities, have told heavily against one of the fundamentals of education, that of continuity." His reports display the deep feeling, that he always had for his pupils, a concern that was not contemporarily recognised or appreciated in return.

By August 1943, the school roll had decreased to 101 pupils and there had been a corresponding withdrawal of teachers back to their own education authorities, who faced with increasing school rolls, were in dire need of teachers.

The reason the mass bombing raids had ceased, was that the Germans had failed to break the population's morale in the mass bombing raids of British cities; although civilian casualties had been heavy at the height of the blitz, sometimes as much as 1000 killed in a night's raid on London. As the bombing stopped, so parents, usually the mother, would want her children home again.

At Clovelly School, the boys still dug for victory, still collected salvage of paper and aluminium from households and on fine days, sitting in the playground, making camouflage netting by threading strips of hessian in different shades and colours through ready made netting. The colours told the more knowledgeable and observant of the children, where the nets were to used, i.e. in Europe or the desert.

In the classroom, the children were always being told how to do without so much paper to write on and all sorts of paper in different colours and texture would be taken into use. Writing books were rationed to one and a quarter books per child per year. Although pencils were in short supply as well, it did not restrain the children too much, as these were the days of nib and ink work. The ink would be made up in a jug with ink powder and water by the ink monitor, then he or she would come around to every desk and fill the ink-well that was sitting in its receptacle in the top of the desk. An ink monitor could always be identified by the horrifically stained hands and fingernails, even a day or so after mixing the stuff . Occasionally, during the filling up procedure, there would be a shout of "Please sir (or Miss), my ink-well is overfilled." This would usually be where the monitor and the particular child did not see eye to eye over some playground problem and the monitor could quite easily pour too much fluid into the ink-well. Consequently, this would usually result in ink spoiled books and guaranteed the resident of the desk to have hands that were similar in hue to the monitor.

It was reported that in the term ending in August 1943, the canteen had served 7330 meals, again, with most of the fruit and vegetables coming from the two gardens that the boys cultivated. Although there was only a small nominal charge to the children for each meal, it was reported that the canteen was making a profit. There was no cost to the canteen for the goods supplied to them. Low wages only would have had to be paid to some of the women who worked there, but many were voluntary helpers. There were no charges involved in producing the crops, other than the seeds, so one can understand that they should have made a profit. I suppose this was paid to the Education Authority, although this was never stated.

By the time 1945 arrived, there were only 93 children on the school roll and in February 1945, Miss Pamela Williams, the teacher from Plymouth, was ordered to return, as she was required to resume teaching at her old school on the 26 February. However, for some unknown reason she did not do so, and it took another letter from the County Education Committee in March, to tell her to return to Plymouth by 10 April. One cannot blame Miss Williams for being reluctant to return to Plymouth, after all, with all its faults and exposure to the elements, Clovelly must be preferable

When V.E. Day came in August 1945, there were very few of the evacuees left in Clovelly and a year later, two still remained locally, Eileen Law, later to become Eileen King, and myself.

CHAPTER TWO

HARRY REMEMBERS

I was born into the Clement family on the day after Trafalgar Day 1929, when the family home was at 248, York Road, Battersea. I was terribly under sized at birth and as I was such a sorry specimen, my parents probably did not expect me to live out the year.

My school was Bellenden Road Elementary School, Peckham, south-east London and my teacher was Mr Bamsey. The Headmaster, a distant and authorative figure was named Mr Cotard and he hailed from either Guernsey or Jersey, in the Channel Islands and from my point of view, his part in my education was to preside over morning assembly in the hall and occasionally (sometimes frequently) administer the severe caning of those whose punishment was deemed greater than that allowed to be administered by class teachers. Those receiving six – eight strokes on each hand, in front of the whole school, already had their names recorded in the Punishment Book, a large black covered tome, and the miscreants name and the punishment awarded would be read out aloud. Mr Cotart would then step forward, swishing his favourite cane and the victim would be ordered to hold out his hand. If the Head and the teachers suspected that there would be trouble from the unfortunate recipient, two or three male teachers would arrange themselves, so as to surround the boy. It was not unusual, in this tough school, to see teachers and boy rolling on the floor, until they could place him across a table for the cane to be administered on his backside. Of course we boys loved all that, especially if we saw that a teacher had been kicked or punched. Usually, Mr Cotard, after giving the beating, would swing around to face us, swishing his cane as if to say, there was plenty of strength left in his arm if anyone else wanted to challenge his authority.

Most of the boys came from financially poor backgrounds and our clothes were normally hand-me-downs or home-made. It was not unusual to see a boy or girl going along to school with a hole in the sole of their boot or shoe (all the boys wore lace-up boots) and that the hole had been covered on the inside by the insertion of a piece of cardboard. If they came from a large family, the cardboard repair was usually indicative that it was not their turn in the family for the father to properly repair the boot/shoe with leather that week.

The authorities did their best perhaps; a number of children in each class, who were considered to be under-nourished, would be called forward each morning by the class teacher and from a large stone jar, dollops of malt would be served directly into the mouth of the child by means of a wooden spatula, which the child took back to his or her desk, licking the last stubborn remains before it had to be discarded in the waste paper basket by the teacher's desk, and the lesson continued.

Such were some of the types of children and their circumstances who attended Bellenden Road Elementary School in the months and weeks approaching September 1939.

Everyone in our family and circle of acquaintances had been discussing the possibility of war for a long time, since 1938 in fact. Perhaps, viewed from the present day, that children as young as nine were talking about whether or not there was to be a war with Germany, would be considered strange, but we children, in our made-up games of fighting, would always have British versus the Germans in battle, perhaps as a result of hearing so much of the First World War (The Great War) from our elders.

So if Germany was going to declare war on Britain, then to us youngsters, that was only to be expected. "We beat 'em last time, so they want to get their own back."

SUNDAY 3rd SEPTEMBER 1939

The Sunday morning that the Prime Minister, Mr Neville Chamberlain was going to speak on the wireless, was fine and sunny but most children would be expected to be indoors to listen to what Mr Chamberlain had to say. We all knew what he looked like as we had seen him many times on the news reel films in the cinema, especially the one where he got out of the 'plane and held up a piece of paper; 'Peace in our time' I believe it was referred to.

The Primes Minister's words coming out of the 'Portadyne' radio were received in silence in our kitchen. My father glared at the radio as if blaming it for the news of war. My mother looked down at the plush table-cloth, biting her lip; her hands held clasped together on the table. For us children the silence that followed was embarrassing but then my dad spoke. Gone was his usual strong forceful style when he said, "Well, so that's it then 'Lot (Charlotte). We're going to have another one."

It was the cue for us children to leave. Mum and Dad were going to have a serious talk and Mum looked as if she was about to cry.

Out in the street, other children were appearing and we eagerly discussed the news and it did not seem very long before the air-raid sirens sounded. Parents rushed from their homes to grab and order children indoors. Of course we had all 'seen' the aircraft in the sky, each claiming they had seen more than anyone else. I just do not know how long we sat in our coal-cellar at 40, Blenheim Grove before Dad considered it safe enough for us to emerge. Later we heard it had all been a false alarm. I was comforted by the thought that I hadn't been shown up by any claim to my peers that I had seen swastikas on any aeroplane.

The weeks that followed saw British troops being sent to France and the topical subject among the children was, "Where's your dad ? Mine's in France."

I remember the winter that year, because of the snow. It appeared to us kids, that it was laying there for weeks on end. It was certainly a long while, because all the excitement and joy that greeted the first fall of snow, disappeared within the first week. Also at this time, my mother had been given, or perhaps she had bought it, some khaki cloth and being a trained seamstress and dressmaker, she made up a complete army uniform for me, even the glengarry hat. I was over the moon, a nine year old walking the streets of Peckham dressed as one of His Majesty's soldiers. My father was not too happy about it though, I remember him saying to my mother, "You needn't worry making him a uniform; he'll be in one soon enough with this war." My father's words were very nearly prophetic, the war ended in September 1945 and I donned the uniform of His Majesty's Grenadier Guards in July 1947.

In the Spring of 1940, Bellenden Road School had some form of evacuation when I discovered that many children had disappeared from school. It transpired that they had been sent to Steyning in Sussex and it has always puzzled me since , why the authorities chose a location nearer to the south coast and which would be reached first by any invading German army coming across the English Channel. Perhaps the reasoning was that the first sight of the pupils of Bellenden Road School would be sufficient to turn-back the Hun vanguard and frighten the clean-living Aryans of the S.S. Panzer Divisions.

I remember that about this time, my brother and I, with our newly purchased haversacks filled and loaded on our backs, were taken by our mother to the courtyard of a college in Peckham Road, I think it was the Art College, and there we saw a line of London double-decker buses drawn along the kerb. There were scores of children, parents and bustling official looking adults with pieces of paper or clip-boards in their hands and looking terribly flustered.

I never did know what happened, but after waiting around for about half an hour, we returned home to our house in Blenheim Grove.

Another go at evacuating us occurred some time later, when the teacher asked how many wished to be evacuated and for us to ask our parents and then give our names to the teacher. When I mentioned this in doors to my mum and dad, it was agreed that I should go but that my brother (four years my senior) would remain at home.

Once again, the making of clothes, buying of small necessities and packing the haversack occupied my mother, who not knowing what date I should be sent away, dealt with the preparations with some haste. When the date was announced at school, it transpired that we only had a day or so before we would all be off to some distant destination, and this was not given out. We were to attend school with our cases, packs, or bags and then we would be taken away. The date given was the 8th, then changed to 14th June 1940. My mother had bought me a small note-book to record things, and I wrote these dates inside the front cover.

The day of departure was fine and sunny and as if reminiscent of the battalions of soldiers who had marched through the streets to war, we children were formed into a long column in ranks of three and marched along Bellenden Road, right into Blenheim Grove, past my house and into Peckham Rye Railway Station.

We did not know where we were going but word filtered down to where I was that we were off to Devonshire. Where? Like many London children whose parents

14

could not afford to take them away on holiday, our bedraggled group had no idea where this was. I remember I called out this information to my mother, who in common with scores of parents, was walking along the pavement beside us. She seemed pleased with our intended destination so I thought, "Well, at least mum knows where I'll be."

Peckham Rye Station was part of the Waterloo Southern Railway system and I remember the train was far longer than the platform, so loading took longer than normal. Teachers, railway staff and police officers, herded us, shouting out instructions of where to go, where to sit and now be quiet. Parents had been kept outside the precinct of the station so there were no embraces and kisses, only the farewells shouted after us, each parent's voice being lost amongst the others.

It was only much later that I was told that my father, who worked on the railway and who had obviously been in a dilemma as to whether my evacuation was the proper course to take, had suddenly thrown down his tools and being within a mile or so along the line from the point of our departure, ran to stop me leaving. He reached the end of the platform as our train was leaving the other end. As he told me subsequently, "Missing that train was the best thing that I did."

I do not recall being frightened. At 10 years of age in wartime London I had grown up quickly. I had older brothers in the services and one had already seen action. At school, we had been taught how to deal with incendiary bombs, working in pairs, with sandbag and stirrup-pump. We children had seen our one piece of greenery – Peckham Rye – dug up with interlaced trenches and air raid shelters, so we thought that we were able to take on the world.

The train journey seemed long and tiring on that warm June day and although it probably stopped a few times en route and maybe at other stations, the first one that I recall was at Exeter Central. Here the platforms were crowded with people, not travellers, but helpers at tables of food and drink for us, the evacuees.

There were ladies to help the younger ones to go to the toilet, for washing etc and to serve them refreshments. Lemonade and tea were provided as well as cakes, sandwiches and other goodies . We were in our element and enjoyed ourselves in this great adventure. It is true to say that at that time, we did not miss our parents. Home sickness would set in at a later stage. Another factor that we, in our excitement, did not realise or appreciate right away, was that we were experiencing our first benefit of the wonderful Devon hospitality. Looking back, I can still see those lovely women, bustling about with plates and glasses and things, saying to one another, "God bless 'em. Poor little things. That damned old Hitler has a lot to answer for."

It is ironical that the departure from Exeter Central Station was more of a farewell than our leaving from Peckham Rye Station. With the crowds of wonderful ladies calling out and waving goodbyes, we children disobeyed railway regulations and the repeated commands of our teachers, when we all leant out of the windows to shout and wave back.

I can still remember the cry echoing along the carriage as one sharp observer was the first to spot the sea. The ensuing rush to that side of the carriage brought more

Crossland Farm

shouted threats from our poor teachers, who by this time, must have been at their wits end with very frayed nerves.

Bideford at last. The platform seemed to be crowded again, but without the tables of food and drink. Very much in evidence though, were the Boy Scouts and the Girl Guides, the Sea Cadets, Boys Brigade and other branches of youth organisations. All the evacuees were ordered to leave the train and as each child stepped down onto the platform, a Scout or Guide or one of the other youngsters, would step forward and take the evacuee's case or pack. Then in a long crocodile, with our local 'helper' walking beside each one of us, we left the station, turned left down the hill, under the

Granny and Granfer Beer

railway bridge, left into Torrington Street and into the Little Bethel Chapel. Upstairs we were led and there in the hall were the tables we were half expecting to see. Each one loaded with food and drink for us. Arrangements had been made for us to be washed and cleaned up before eating and then after we had demolished the food etc we were split up for the first time.

16

I think it was at that moment that the great adventure started to lose its appeal. Some of the evacuees went off in buses and I saw them later at school. Others went off and I never met up with them again. These were my companions from the Bellenden Road School as well as others from a separate school; my friends on the evacuation. A group of us were seen by a doctor and then without anything being said to us, we were put to one side, whilst the important looking adults talked to each other, with just an occasional look at us.

Eventually, my little group were led out into the street again. We did not know where we were going or what was happening. Our erstwhile 'helpers' had by this time, gone, so we had to carry our own cases, packs and parcels, but it was not too far before we were ushered into a house at Springfield Terrace, which overlooked the River Torridge. The house seemed full of children and was consequently, very noisy. After we had been taken to the rooms we were to occupy, three or four beds to a room, we were all called into a downstairs room where we were given a bit of pencil, a piece of paper and an envelope, with instructions to write to our parents to say we had arrived safely and to give the Springfield Terrace address. This was the first letter I had ever written to my parents and I cannot now recall what it contained. No doubt describing the train journey, the food and pop drinks given to us, then repeating the part about the food etc.

I was only at Springfield Terrace for a day or so when a few of us were told to pack again and come downstairs. More farewells, to our new found friends before travelling by bus to the village of Parkham. Here our new home was to be the Rectory (now known as the Old Rectory) and we found a few children from another London school already ensconced.

It was at Parkham, that I first met up with another kind of Devonshire greeting; stoning by the local boys whenever we ventured to step outside the gate into the lane. Even in the garden, we were not safe, as the stones came over the wall. I thought this was wrong as we had not done anything against the locals, and eventually, although we were not a real gang of friends of long standing, we were London children from a fairly tough neighbourhood and extremely streetwise. Most had been brought up in pretty poor areas of London where one had to be tough and fight for what you believed in to exist. So the gate was opened and as we stepped out, our little gang of perhaps half a dozen boys, received a shower of good Devon rock. Shouting at the top of our voices, we charged the local boys and got to grips with them. Street urchins are dirty fighters and it was all over in a few minutes and the local kids ran away as fast as their hobnailed boots would allow them. For the rest of our stay, we received nothing more harmful than verbal abuse, hurled from a safe distance at the end of the lane.

Our next journey was only a short one, this time to Clovelly Court. The weather was still summery and warm so it was no hardship to wait on the lawn whilst some ladies fussed over us. I remember that I thought that they spoke rather posh and a lot different to the mothers of those with whom I had gone to school. I learned later that this was the Hon. Mrs Betty Asquith, the Misses Leeke and one or two other ladies whose names I now forget.

Soon, some other ladies came over to us, looked at us, some pointed at this or that child, there was some discussion held quietly between one or the other of the Leekes and, as it turned out, one of the ladies from the village, and this or that child would be taken off to their new home. One rather plump lady, was shaking her head when obviously being offered a brother and sister of about thirteen and six respectively. Instead, she walked over to where I was now standing alone, nodded her head and then held out her hand

Wrinkleberry School 1940

for me. I took it and she took my pack as she started to lead me away. However, one Miss Leeke, I do not know which one, took us in her little open tourer motor car up to my new home, Crossland Farm. I was told later, that when this lady was offered the brother and sister, she was told that the boy was "big and strong and able to help on the farm", but that she had replied, "I'm not taking the maid, I don't want the bother of a little maid."

Annie and Bill Beer were everything that wonderful people should be. Right from the moment she took my hand, I felt someone who was loving and kind. She made me happy again, although I was in a strange place with strange people, her very touch comforted me. Walking into her shadowy kitchen, I met her husband. His twinkling blue eyes, white hair and matching moustache oozed friendship, just like one's favourite uncle. They were both in their sixties – in fact both Granny and Granfer (this was how I was to know them for the rest of their lives) was drawing their pensions, with Granny being a year older than Granfer, as he was always reminding me.

Straight away, I was sat down to the table, a large slice of fruit cake and a glass of real milk was placed in front of me. "Get stuck in boy, it'll do you good" she said. I finished the milk quickly and was amazed when she re-filled the glass. Coming from the social background that was my lot, very few people had real milk; our milk came out of tins and was sweet. Tins of condensed milk was the norm in most families that I knew; it went further and without refrigerators, kept even in the hottest of summers.

It was whilst I sat there, that the Miss Leeke, who had driven us up from Court House, returned, and came to the door. She had brought a rubber sheet to be put on the bed in case I wet it. I do not know exactly what was said but I heard Annie Beer's

18

voice saying, "No thank you Miss Leeke. If the boy wets the bed it doesn't matter. It's only to be expected after what he's been through. No, if he wets the bed I'll wash it."

I did not wet the bed, thereby underlining Annie Beer's confidence in me.

Later, I was to discover that although I and many others had been fortunate to have wonderful people as foster parents in Clovelly, some, mercifully only a few, had been billeted with people who made the child's life a misery. In most instances the miserable child eventually disclosed all and was moved to someone with more Christian feeling.

Having experienced such wonderful friendship and hospitality from Devon folk, it was a great shock to me recently, in reading through the old copies of the Bideford & North Devon Gazette held in the North Devon Record Office. According to the report published in the newspaper the week following our arrival, some 4000 evacuees were sent from London to the Torridgeside area of North Devon and, "…owing to insufficient responses to the voluntary billeting appeal some compulsory powers had to be used." The columnist 'Torridge Chat' wrote "…occasionally, in the talking groups, I heard expressions of opinion of which the speakers ought to have been ashamed. But there was a goodness of heart that far outweighed any other feeling that might have crept in. After all the youngsters who had been evacuated could not help coming here…." I still like to think that those selfish individuals who refused to consider the plight of others, especially children, were very much in the minority.

Clovelly had been crowded with evacuees from my school and another group from Evelyn Street School, Deptford, and of course, Clovelly village school at Wrinkleberry, was not equipped to take approximately 160 extra pupils, so until some alterations could be done, it was a case of finding a barn if it was wet or if fine and dry, the fields and lanes would do for our school.

As it happened, our own London teachers would take us for walks in the lanes, fields and woods, then halting us, would commence a spellingbee, or subject us to mental arithmetic, in fact any educational subject that did not require books. One barn that was a regular shelter for us, was an old cob barn at East Dyke Farm, which Mr J.C. Hilton was kind enough to let us use. I remember we children standing around the walls of the barn whilst the teacher dwelt on the subject in hand. Although I later caught up with the rest of my formal education, those early days of rudimentary schooling taught me a lot; mental arithmetic and spelling have been my best subjects ever since.

Some few weeks after being evacuated, my mother and father came down for the week-end and stayed at Crossland. They wanted to satisfy themselves that I was happy and that I was being well cared for. I know their feelings about Granny and Granfer Beer because as my father was saying goodbye to me, he gave me some sound words of advice. "Behave yourself son, they're good people and they will look after you. Just you behave yourself." I suppose that they could see that Granny and Granfer Beer were coping well with me and were giving me a good home.

Just in time before the cold weather came, we were told we could be accommodated in the school,(according to records, the evacuees were merged with the Clovelly children in the school on 20th September 1940) and so we joined in with the local children, making mixed classes. There was no separation between Londoners and locals, which was one of the best things the authorities ruled on, as it helped us to merge into village life, that is, those of us that wished to. The Head Teacher was Mr R.K. Hesketh, Miss Barbara Cruse taught the infants, whilst our own teachers Miss Place, Mr Bamsey and Miss Woods taught other classes. Another teacher was later sent to help out at the school, but I cannot remember her name. There was another school for the younger evacuees in the village (down the cobbles) and this was the old chapel of St. Peters.

There was very little privacy from one class to another in the hall, as the partitions had been made with curtains so whilst one class would be wrestling with dictation, the next class would loudly recite a multiplication table. Still we managed and survived.

Sadly some of the evacuees started to return to London after only a few months away, and perhaps we could be forgiven for being heartless in thinking that at least this gave us more room in school.

It was about this time that I received salutary punishment for a minor misdemeanour, but the subsequent events which culminated were far greater than either the misdemeanour or punishment. My class was having a singing/music lesson and I was obviously playing about and not giving due attention to the lesson, when I was caught by Miss Woods. I make no excuses for my behaviour, I was probably a terror and if the roles had been reversed, I would possibly have ended up in prison for an assault on the child.

Miss Wood, at that moment, was milder in her reaction to my naughtiness than she deserved to be; she merely instructed me to come out in front of the class, facing the wall near to where she was playing the piano. Right beside me was one of the large Tortoise stoves that burnt coke and it stood on a sheet of metal. Lying on the sheet of metal was the metal poker and against the wall, within the guard-rails, was a heavy wooden poker. Trying to be helpful (or was I) I picked up the metal poker and stood it alongside its wooden companion, but I had not reckoned with the vibration that the playing of the piano caused to the floorboards and which was relayed through to the metal sheet. Of course, the obvious happened and the metal poker fell to the floor with a crash.

Miss Woods stopped playing the piano, the children started to laugh and quick as a flash, no doubt at the very end of her tether as far as I was concerned, Miss Woods turned, picked up the wooden poker and hit me right across the top of my head with sufficient force to take me to my knees.

She helped me up and sent me back to my seat but I do not recall the rest of the lessons that day. No doubt the poor woman was shattered, firstly by my behaviour and then the result of her temper: I am grateful she had enough sense to choose the wooden poker rather than the metal one.

When I arrived back at Crossland Farm at the end of the days schooling, Grannie Beer (I had taken to calling Annie and Bill Beer by the affectionate and well suited title of Grannie and Granfer) created a big fuss and when Granfer came in they discussed the matter and resolved that being legally responsible for my welfare, they would take the matter further. Accordingly, the next morning, before lessons, Granfer Beer had his say with Mr Hesketh.

He accepted Mr Hesketh's opinion that I was no angel, but insisted that the punishment was excessive. The wound on my head was there for anyone to see for several days afterwards, in fact it was still apparent after Miss Woods had suddenly and without notice left our school, and it was said, returned to London.

I have often thought about this incident and hope, that as the bombing of London was at its worst, she did not return to get hurt in a raid, all because of a stupid boy; but then, perhaps she felt she would rather face Hitler's bombs than the antics of a ten year old boy called Harry Clement.

We found that the reception from the Clovelly children was much more friendlier than that of their Parkham neighbours. Like all schoolboys we formed 'gangs' and at Wrinkleberry they were always a mixture of local and evacuees. One of the games we later played in the playground was Stalingrad where a group of seven or eight of us would defend a corner of the yard and all the rest of the boys who wished to join in this extremely rough game, would attempt to capture the corner. It was a very physical affair with punches being liberally exchanged between the two groups. The attackers of course were the Germans and we were the Russians. We 'Russians' always took as many of the Russian general's names that we knew, such as Timoshenko; Voroshilov; Zhukov; Budenny and Koniev,as our own. I know that I was always Marshall Timoshenko and fought in the first line of defenders. Sometimes our defence was so physical that the attackers numbers rapidly diminished and we would always win. I think that many of my peers came to regard it as a test of endurance and physical pain.

The term evacuees was a new word to most of us and it was used liberally and on most occasions, instead of Londoners.

Some of those local children who I went to school with so long ago, still stand out in my memory. Caleb Jennings and his two sisters; Mary Littlejohns; Hilda Braund; Sheila Ellis and her brother John; Phyllis Cook and her two brothers, Roy and Ken; John Westlake, who walked all the way to school from Stitworthy; Molly Beer, who likewise travelled a good way – from Mettaford Cottages at one time;Jim Whitefield; Tommy Cruse; Bernard Abbot ; Doreen Braund; Bill, Les and Ken Rowe. From nearer home,(my Clovelly home) I remember Norman Headon, Brian Taylor, Margaret Bragg and her sisters; Fred Robins and George Smith; Ruth Jewell from Burscott, Margaret and Florence Jewell from Hugglepit Cottage.

On the subject of Wrinkleberry School, I remember the dentist coming to visit the school once. He was accompanied by a nurse; I shall always have in my mind's eye that she was big and powerful. Presently it was my turn to go into this classroom that had been emptied for its use as a surgery. Well, the dentist decided that I had to have a tooth drilled and filled and I remember he used a machine that he pedalled with one foot and this drove the drill. With the matter dealt with, I was sent back to my class to continue whatever we were doing. By the time 'playtime' came around, my face was swelling and the tooth was aching considerably. As we were leaving our desks, Mr Hesketh asked what was the matter and I told him. He opened the door to the surgery' and informed them that my tooth was hurting. The dentist nodded, indicated the chair (an ordinary school chair) and as I sat in it, I was grasped by the powerful nurse and held whilst the dentist, without any preliminaries, yanked out the offending tooth. I would not have minded perhaps, except that the tooth had not been giving me any trouble prior to his 'treatment'.

School photograph taken at Wrinkleberry, Higher Clovelly.
Harry Clement in 1941

Mr Hesketh had fought in the Great War of 1914-18 and often used to relate stories of what he had seen and gone through whilst serving in the Grenadier Guards and then in the Guards Machine Gun Corps. This was right up my street in interest and if ever, during a dull or hated lesson, I or a few of the others, could turn the lesson to the subject of the Germans or the Guards, we would have Mr Hesketh talking about the first battle of Loos or the Somme in no time. When General Alexander took command in the Mediterranean area, Mr Hesketh told us about how 'Alex' had been his platoon commander and what a super chap he was. At that time, little did I know that one day I would join the Grenadier Guards and later meet my idol, 'Alex'.

This was the age of the horse and I was to see plenty of them, working in the fields and my first sight of the gathering of the corn harvest. Although a "nisseldraft" (Devon dialect for 'runt') when I first arrived, Grannie and Granfer Beer had made sure that I had plenty of cream and raw milk every day to build me up (a glass of warm milk straight from the cow at morning and afternoon milkings and a dish of scalded cream every day), so hard work was the next thing to promote my growth. That first corn harvest I found out and appreciated what Devonshire dashels (thistles) were, but what I did not know was that they would be far worse when dried by the time the corn came to be threshed and the prickles had dried to needle-like toughness.

I was also taught to hand milk by Granfer Beer and he selected an older cow who he said was a hard milker, if I could milk her then I would be able to milk the others.

This meant nothing to me until Granfer explained that some cows 'held' their milk and this made it harder to draw milk from them. He told me that I would probably see people on other farms doing what was called 'wet milking', that was squirting some milk from the teat into the palm of the hands, rubbing the hands together and then milking. Consequently, drips of excess milk on the hand could fall into the milk bucket and Granfer Beer's view (since confirmed by hygienists) was that this was a dirty way to go about things, "If you can't milk dry, then don't milk at all" was his doctrine.

If it was the time of the horse on the farms, it was also the time of small farms in the Clovelly parish. In the early 1940's there were about thirteen or fourteen small farms between the bottom of Slerra Hill and Dyke Green, some with no more than a couple of fields and maybe two to three cows. It was also the time when farmers helped one another with their harvesting and later, the threshing. A days work by a man would be repaid when he needed some help. Likewise, it was sometimes possible, if a farmer only had one horse, to borrow one from a friend, to make up a team.

In February 1941, forty Bristol children arrived to take up any spare room in our bulging school. It is possible that at this time, Mr Hesketh was in charge of a school of some 200 pupils, most of whom were 'foreigners'. In May 1941, another group of evacuees were landed on Clovelly. They came from Plymouth when that city was bombed; but I suppose the saving grace as far as Mr Hesketh was concerned, was that both the Bristol and Plymouth groups brought with them their own teachers; Miss Howell came from Bristol, while Miss Williams came from Plymouth.

One of the many additional things that occurred in Clovelly directly because of the war, was that in May 1941 the Education authorities leased the Rectory stable block and coach-house and converted them into a school canteen, so that the evacuees could be fed at lunch times. During the first term that it was in use the voluntary staff served some 7000 dinners. Granny Beer told me, "I don't hold with such things boy, there'll be a meal here for you so you don't need to go down there."

Most of the vegetables came from two gardens which we older children dug, planted and then harvested. I can honestly say, that I never did taste anything that I grew from my sections of the gardens, although plenty was harvested.

It was during a spell of gardening that I received another minor punishment. Another evacuee, who did not have the advantage of a Granfer Beer as his foster father (he had been deputy head gardener at Court House gardens) had enquired of me if I had any seeds he could put in his patch of the garden. I replied that I would get him some. Subsequently, I gave his a matchbox filled with seeds that looked like brussels sprout seeds, which I claimed they were. He planted them nicely in a row and when they came up, and as he was admiring them, Mr Hesketh approached him and asked what did he think he was doing, sowing weeds in the garden. Of course he told the Head that Harry Clement had given them to him as brussels sprouts and I was summarily dealt with around the ear and then instructed to hoe the other boy's patch. I cannot help remembering this incident everytime I see the seed pods of Red Campions (Red Robins).

Wrinkleberry School had quite a good record educationally and it was always said, that at one time, most of the ships masters in the White Star and Cunard Lines had come from Clovelly, having been educated at the school. Among a few people it was known in a jocular fashion as 'Wrinkleberry College'.

Granfer Beer always referred to it by that name and it stood me in good stead later on in my life. It happened in 1954 when I was approached to take a trial with the fashionable Harlequins Rugby Club and when I swiftly agreed, arrangements were made for me to be at Harlequins H.Q. at the Stoop Memorial Ground at Teddington.

There were only two of us to be taking a trial, a young RAF lad and myself. The players were a great bunch of men, most of whom I had seen before, but merely their photographs in newspapers. Some of the club officials were very pompous and didn't have much time for either the RAF chap or myself. There came a point after we had had quite a few runs and passes and we were having a break, that my fellow trialist asked me if the club officials had asked me what school I had attended. I replied that they had and that I had told them quite truthfully that I had been educated at Wrinkleberry College and that when an official had somewhat disdainfully asked where that was, I had told him it was in the West Country, a fact that had satisfied him. Subsequently, I was accepted and played for what I considered to be the best rugby club in the country.

In the warm weather, a lot of the children went down to the beach to play in the Quay pool and whilst many of them were getting their swimming proficiency certificates, I was home at Crossland, learning farming and gardening.

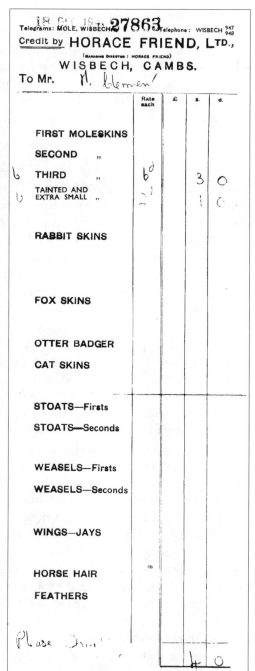

Invoice for my moleskins

I soon learnt ways of augmenting the small amount of pocket money (one shilling) that my mother sent wrapped in her letter to me every week. In the summer I would help out at hay harvest and later the corn harvest, for which I would earn a few shillings from Granfer and a neighbouring farmer – Tommy Squires of Hugglepit. There was also potato picking to be done; a back tiring job, but it brought in the shillings. In the winter, I trapped moles and rabbits, and occasionally – by accident – I caught stoats as well. All these would be skinned and nailed stretched out on boards in the loft above the cow shippon. When the skins were well and truly dried – and here Granfer Beer would advise me – I would send them off to Horace Friends & Co.Ltd at Wisbech, in Cambridgeshire, hoping that I would make my fortune on what I considered to be Grade 1 skins. Alas, everytime I received my Postal Orders in payment, my efforts had been classed as Grade 2 or 3. Horse hair from the regular grooming was also another source of money from Horace Friend, although he only offered the best prices for very long hair cut from the manes and tails – something neither Granfer nor I were prepared to do.

All my savings went into my Post Office Saving Bank book which was numbered Higher Clovelly No.9. This is still in my possession and when I look back through it today, I marvel at the minute amounts that I carried up to Hester and Harry Taylor's post office/shop for them to enter into my growing account.

Employment Card

This was a time of occasional German bombing raids on Cardiff and Swansea and at times you could hear bombers going over at night and knew not whether they were friend or foe, but there was always folk that would say, "They're Gerry, you can hear the engines sound different, you know, boom, boom boom." A daily occurrence would be the long convoys of ships sailing past Clovelly and many times I watched as planes flew around the ships and dived at them, occasionally hearing the gunfire but watching for the puffs of smoke in the air to denote exploding anti-aircraft shells. I remember watching British fighter aircraft attacking the German bombers, and once I saw the Germans attacked by American built P.38 Lightning's which came screaming across the bay.

Harry Clement with Ben at Crossland Farm 1942

One night, 24th August 1943, I shall always remember, when Granny came banging on my bedroom door and shouting. "Get up boy, there's bombs dropping" Quickly getting out of bed and fumbling to put my clothes on in the dark, although it was not yet midnight, I could hear Granny and Granfer talking very loudly, Granny was downstairs and Granfer was still getting dressed. Within a minute I was leaving the bedroom, and as I passed the back window at the bottom of the stairs, I saw a huge red glow from a fire that appeared to be near at hand.

Harry Clement at Crossland Farm 1942

Going into the kitchen I saw that Grannie had her coat on over her nightie and she was wearing her outdoor shoes, and something I had never seen before, was that she had her hair done up in plaits. She was very agitated that Granfer was taking so long to come downstairs and when he did appear she suggested that he go out to see what was happening. All this while, the only light that we had in the kitchen was the torch that Granny had placed on the table.

As soon as the back door was open, ignoring commands to stay inside, I was out with Granfer and looking towards where the flames denoted an obvious fire. Our instant opinion was that it was neighbouring West Dyke Farm that was ablaze, but our view was restricted by the field hedge and before anyone could stop me, I ran and climbed up onto the garden hedge to give myself a better view. From here I could see across two fields to West Dyke farm and could clearly see the flames glittering on the window panes of the farmhouse. This showed me that the fire was in the field in front of the house from where I looked.

We still did not know what had happened but Granny had said that she was woken up by a loud bang and the bedroom window burst open and a huge conch shell, that she had on the window sill for years, came flying across the room and landed on the bed. Whilst we were downstairs, there were one or two other explosions and Granny was convinced that we were being bombed.

As we stood out in the field we could hear other noises now, an occasional dull explosion and the cracking sound of bullets being discharged. Being a young know-all, I proclaimed that it was a crashed German plane and its bombs and bullets were going off. This was enough for Granny to sweep both Granfer and myself into the house, whereupon she locked the door and proceeded to make a pot of tea.

Early the next morning I went out with Granfer to see what had happened. As we walked up the main road (Slerra) from Crossland, we saw that the telephone wires had been torn from the poles and were strewn across the roadway. At Turn Pike, which was the junction with a small lane – known as Shop Lane – that led to Hugglepit and Hartland, we saw the barge-board of the Stoop Farmhouse was lying in the front garden, and along Shop Lane we were surprised to see a lot of loose thatch lying in the front yard of the thatched shop. Looking up to the roof we could see a large gouge across the front (east side) of the thatched roof. On the opposite side of the lane, we saw that the tops had been cut off the small trees on the high hedge.

We walked another twenty yards or so and saw lorries and RAF and Army personnel working in the field at Hugglepit Cross. Standing in the middle of the road was the village policeman, Mr West. Straight away he said to Granfer, "Where were you last night Beer, you didn't come here then." Granfer looked up into the policeman's face and replied very quietly, "Mr Churchill said that if anything unusual was to happen you must stay put, and that was what I did."

Mr West just snorted and turned away; he did not know Granfer like I did. Granfer might have answered quietly and calmly but I knew from his lovely blue eyes that he was blazing mad with the policeman's stupid remark. The scene was one of devastation, with red soil mingling with running water – for it had been bad weather over the last few days – and resulting in a foot clinging mess. With so many vehicles and feet tramping through it, the mud was soon spread over a large area of roadway.

I subsequently learnt that the aircraft was a Wellington bomber No.MP624, from Chivenor air base, across the Bay from Clovelly and its crew, ranging in rank from Wing Cdr. to Flight Sergeant, had all lost their lives in the crash. Later that morning, they carried the bodies along to the policeman's garage and laid them on the floor, then covered them with a tarpaulin. I remember seeing the tarpaulin with a row of boots sticking out at the bottom when I went along to the policeman's house to deliver his milk at eight o'clock.

The policeman was not my most favourite man in the village although his wife was a lovely lady. I used to deliver a pint of fresh milk that had just come from the cow, every morning to the policeman's house and also every evening as well. One day I tripped on the stone steps coming up from his front gate and dropped a sixpence that

I held in my hand. I was so concerned in not spilling the milk that the coin went flying into the grass beside the path. He was digging in his garden at the time and shouted across to me to stop what I was doing. When I tried to explain what had happened, he repeated his order, and when he shouted you obeyed smartly. I was about to put this sixpence into my Post Office saving account and now that I had lost it brought me almost to tears. I remember that Mrs West had seen or heard something of what went on, for when I took the can of milk to her back door, she looked down the garden to where her husband was digging and asked what had I lost. When I told her she went and fetched me a sixpence, telling me not to tell anyone about it. I have often wondered whether that sixpence came out of one of her husband's pockets.

When I was a bit older, I used to deliver Mr West's annual load of farmyard dung for his garden. This had to be forked OVER the top of his fuschia hedge and woe betide me if there was one trace of the farmyard draped on his bushes. There was never a word of thanks from him and it was always a mystery to me about his payment for this and other things he had.

Before I was thirteen years of age Granfer Beer had taught me to fire a 12-bore shotgun, including all the attendant cautions. He was a first class coach and I had watched him closely everytime he had shot anything, in fact I aped his actions completely. Also around about this time, I had been taught to drive a tractor. Tommy Squires, who farmed Hugglepit, had bought a new Fordson tractor, which had spade-lug wheels instead of the rubber tyred model and was terribly hard for a young boy to steer. To turn the steering wheel, particularly when in soft ground, often needed more muscle than a boy had and to depress the clutch pedal was an effort which I remember to this day. The first time I drove it, I made a bodge of trying to turn from the lane into the lower yard at Hugglepit. Seeing that I did not have sufficient lock on the wheels to negotiate the gateway, I stopped before I removed a gatepost. Dear old Tommy got me to stand on the clutch whilst he yanked the long gear lever into reverse and between us the tractor was driven into the yard. Everytime I go through this gate now, my mind flashes back to that day and the sweat I was in at the time.

To assist in the war effort, school children everywhere were encouraged to do their bit. When 'Salvage Week' regularly came around, we children would visit even the remotest farms to collect any unwanted scrap metal that we could get into hand carts or sledges. Collecting newspapers and rags were also areas we were employed in to assist. I remember being taught with some other older children, how to weave coloured strips of hessian through huge rope nets. We were told they were for camouflaging tanks, guns and lorries and we older boys always knew when we were making nets up for the desert, as the strips were sand coloured.

Another measure that was introduced by the authorities was to allow school children of a certain age to work a limited number of hours on the land during hay, corn and potato harvests. Those of us that opted to be allowed to do such workwere issued with a blue employment card, which had to be taken with us to the farm we were working on and the farmer had to write down the number of hours we worked and the date and then sign it. I still have mine and it appears so very formal today, but at least the education authorities were attempting to keep us from exploitation.

In those days, potato digging was mostly done by potato-diggers drawn by a pair of horses. This spun the potatoes out of the ground but they then had to be picked by hand and bagged. It was no job for anyone with a weak back or was worried about the state of their hands. The going rate of pay was sixpence an hour and if you stuck a week of it, you had a princely sum to be added to the post office savings account.

Granfer Beer was one of about four farmers who delivered milk down to the village and the milk was conveyed in large stainless milk churns, that held four gallons, and they were suspended by chains from a wooden yoke worn across the shoulders. I watched Granfer do this on the many occasions that I accompanied him and then came the day when as we were returning up the cobbles he asked if I wanted to carry the empty churns. Wearing the yoke was another first for me and I felt ten feet tall.

Little did I know that a few years later, when Granfer was ill, I was given the responsibility of delivering the milk to our several customers in the village. I was petrified of slipping on the cobbles and spilling the milk, and having to apologise to the customers that their milk was running down past their cottages, and what would I have told Granny. Although I had one or two near misses on wet days, I never did slip and spill any milk.

There was a wonderful relationship between the farming and fishing community in those days and occasionally to relieve a predominating fish diet, Granfer, as well as the other milk suppliers, would carry down rabbits, all wrapped up and slung from the chains of the yoke and given to chosen customers. Invariably, fish would be given in exchange a few days later and helped out our diet.

According to the records, by the end of August 1943, the number of pupils in the school had dropped to 101. Miss Woods had already returned and in 1942, Miss Howells of Bristol returned, Miss Place and Mr Bamsey followed in 1943.

I went back to London for two weeks at Christmas in 1943. My mum and my eldest sister, who had just lost her husband in a U-boat attack, came to meet me at Waterloo Railway Station. I had gone away from London, a weak looking little specimen and had returned (albeit briefly) three years later, strong, tanned and standing five feet nine inches tall. I was amazed at what had happened to London, old familiar landmarks and streets were gone; the streets surrounding my first school in Battersea, had been laid flat, in fact it was a vast open space.

My first night in London was remarkable in that I was wakened by the sound of an air-raid siren. My brother Tony, with whom I shared a double bed, was home on leave from the Royal Navy, but as I listened to the siren I realised that he was still fast asleep. Thinking I was doing the correct thing, I elbowed him in the back and then told him the sirens were sounding. His remarks taught me a few words I had never heard before and he rolled over and went asleep again.

At fourteen years of age, Caleb Jennings, Eileen Law and I left school at the Christmas break, but I was not destined to return home to London. As far as I was

29

concerned, I was a part of Clovelly and I wanted to stay. So I worked with Granfer Beer on his small Crossland Farm (the house is now 143, Slerra) whilst most of the other evacuees had gone home. The only one that left London with me that June day in 1940 and still remained, was Eileen Law, now Eileen King and living in Bideford, in North Devon.

It was arranged that I should go home again to London for Christmas. This was 1944 and the regular German bombing raids had finished but London and some southern counties were suffering the horror of attacks by German V1 'flying bombs' and V2 rockets. About the second evening at home, I was having a meal of scrambled (dried egg powder) egg on toast with my mother, sister and brother-in-law, when suddenly there was a huge bang, the windows nearly came in and the room moved about. Most of us stopped eating, forks poised before open mouths and I noticed that my sister had gone white. My mother looked down at the table and said, "Some poor souls have just gone ". I could then see why the V2 was called Hitler's terror weapon, no warning, just death if you happened to be within a street of where it landed.

The next morning I had to see where it had hit and found the site only a few streets from my mum's home. I couldn't believe the depth of the crater, I swear two London buses or trams could have been placed end to end within the crater. At the end of two weeks, the extra food I had taken up to my mother had been exhausted and it would have been unfair to stay longer and eat their rations, so back to Clovelly I returned.

By this time I could do most things on a farm, from hedging to thatching hay and corn ricks. I had learnt to handle a pair of horses in farm implements and work with them all day. I had worked in most positions around a threshing machine and achieved my goal, when one day it was suggested that I go up on top of the threshing machine and cut the bindings ('bean' in local dialect) on the sheaves of corn that were being pitched from the corn rick. I was asked if I had a knife and was it safe. I produced mine, already with a piece of binder twine attached to its swivel with which I could tie it to my wrist. It was important that the knife did not fall into the hopper with the sheaves, not only to protect the machinery, but to protect the 'feeder' and myself as it would most probably fly out at us when it hit the internal blades.

I worked on the farm until July 1947 when I was 17 years of age, and then I joined the Grenadier Guards.

I have never lost touch with Clovelly or its people, because I came back at every leave whilst in the Guards and every year afterwards. My children, who first came down here in their carry-cots, have since, brought their children to this area. It was no misjudgement on my part, that when I left the Metropolitan Police at New Scotland Yard, I returned home to Clovelly, so that I could relive my many memories and to be close to dear old 'Wrinkleberry College' and my friends.

CHAPTER THREE

ROSIE'S TALE

In 1940, my name was Rose Cooper and these are some memories of my evacuation.

Deptford, in South London, is an area that borders the south bank of the River Thames at the point where the river makes a big southern turn and then almost immediately turns north again before continuing its passage eastwards. Deptford is opposite to the Isle of Dogs and Millwall on the north side of the river, lies west of Greenwich and east of Bermonsey.

Before the war, most of the riverside was taken up with wharves and huge black grimed warehouses with narrows streets. Then came the rows of small terrace houses and corner shops. It was typical of London's docklands that the dock workers were housed close to their work (when work was available) and each small group of streets became a village in itself, with friendships, marriages and local feuds being contained in the tiny district in very much the same as in a rural village.

The men would drink in their favourite local pub, their wives would shop in the most convenient local shops and the children would go to the nearest L.C.C. school. Within such a borough as Deptford, there would be more than a few of these small 'villages'. In my area, Evelyn Street Elementary School was where we were educated and from where, those who passed their exams and whose parents could afford it, went on to the Grammar School. For most of us though, it meant that at fourteen years of age we left school to go to work to help out on the family budget.

Before the war I lived with my mum and dad and brother George in a flat above the general stores that my parents (Rose and Ernie) had in Grove Road. My dad had bought the general stores with the compensation he received after an terrible accident. He had been employed as a steel erector (spiderman) and whilst at work had fallen over sixty feet, suffered horrible injuries and had spent a year in hospital. Just before war was declared in 1939, I left school and my mum had another son, Ernie.

It was obvious to most people that if Hitler's bombers came over London, then they would most certainly bomb the docks and that also meant that the streets of little terrace houses and shops, packed row upon row near to the wharves, would also get hit, and that would mean many casualties. Most people who went to the cinema had seen what bombing could do to cities as we had seen the newsreel films of the bombing of cities in China, Spain and Poland.

Everywhere around the area they were digging trenches and air-raid shelters, putting sandbag walls around public buildings and masking windows with sticky tape. The blackout regulations had started and that meant that we all had to get our windows covered when we lit the lights at night. Usually this was heavy black cloth curtains that the families made up and hung over the window every night. More and more people appeared in uniform, more and more men were getting called-up for the Services but my dad, because of the injuries he was still suffering from, could not be considered for the Services.

When it was announced that the government were going to evacuate thousands of school children from London to the countryside, my mum and dad were not too keen at all, as my dad put it, "Rose my love, if it happens that we get killed, I'd prefer it that we were all together and not leave him without us." However, I think it was my mum who had the final say, as she usually did, and George's name was put down on the school list to go.

In June 1940, George went off with a lot of other children from Evelyn Street School in buses to Peckham Rye Station where they caught the train with a lot of Peckham children and were taken down to Devonshire. My mum and dad subsequently got a letter from him saying that he was in a village called Clovelly in North Devon and that he was staying with a Mr & Mrs Cruse in Star Cottage. George used to write every week and he used to tell us about Clovelly and it sounded a lovely place. As the bombing started in London, Hitler proved many people right by

"Lookout" and "Lookout Cottage", Clovelly

hitting at the docks and of course this was reported in some form in the newspapers. No doubt Mrs Cruse saw it and wrote to my parents to say that if the bombing got any worse, we should consider moving down to Clovelly. She thought that there was a chance of an empty cottage that could be rented from Clovelly Estate, who owned Clovelly.

Again there was a family discussion about moving out of London and this time my dad had the final say. I remember him on the platform at Waterloo railway station as my mum, baby brother and me said goodbye. We all shed a lot of tears as we hugged each other, not knowing if we should ever see one another again. It was arranged that dad would send some furniture down by goods train as the cottage we were to live in was absolutely bare.

We arrived at Bideford in the dark after eight hours of travelling by train. Somehow, in the blackout in a strange place, mum carrying baby Ernie and a suitcase and me carrying two suitcases, we found a bus that would take us to Clovelly. I remember the conductor's name was Gordon (Gordon Perham) and he was very helpful to us. When we arrived at Clovelly in pouring rain, we were met by Mrs Cruse and one of her daughters named Rachael.

Now we had no idea what Clovelly was like, we knew nothing of the steep cobbled street that was for

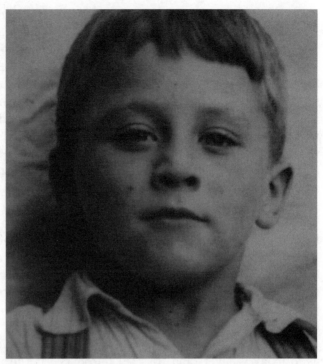

George Cooper aged seven years. 1941

pedestrians and donkeys only and of course neither my mum or I wore suitable shoes for the cobbles. Mrs Cruse took my mum's right arm, I held to my mum's left arm and Rachael held my left arm. Between us we carried the luggage and Ernie was carried by my mum. Pitch black, pouring rain and walking down a very steep cobbled street that we did not know and could not see is something that I shall always remember. Usually, newcomers to Clovelly see the wonder of the beautiful street as they turn the first corner. They can look down as the street wanders down between the cottages to the harbour. All this was denied to us. I was sure that we were walking into the sea and I turned to my mum and said as much, but she replied "Don't talk silly and shut up."

At last we reached Mrs Cruse's home in Star Cottage and there waiting for us was my brother George. The tears rolled down our cheeks as we hugged and kissed each other, we were happy to see him and he was happy to see us. Oh, it was such a happy re-union and with the exception of my dad, we were a family again. Then it was up to our rooms to get changed into dry clothes, as we were soaking wet through after our sliding and staggering walk down from the bus. When we came downstairs, there being put out on the table, was a wonderful hot meal that Mrs Cruse had prepared for us and were we ready for it.

Soon we were lovely and warm, all chatting to one another and once the meal was finished we could feel the effects of the long day. Mum got baby Ernie ready and put him to bed, then it was George's turn, even though he was so excited, and I was not long in following them upstairs. I tried to see through the window to what sort of village it was, but of course it was very dark and I could not see anything. I lay awake for a bit, listening to the waves rolling up on the beach and then sleep took over.

The 'local alarm clock' woke me up in the morning and I opened my eyes to see sea-gulls flying past the window, screeching as only they can. Quickly jumping out of bed, I rushed to the window and looked out. There below me was the sea, and I could see the tiny harbour of Clovelly, with its stone quay, fishermen in boats or on the quay, fishing nets, fish in baskets ready to be taken away and further across were red cliffs with trees on top. There was so much to be absorbed in that first look and oh how wonderful it felt. I had always been used to looking out of windows onto other buildings, at the front, back, and sides, but here there seemed to be only a few houses across from us and I could see the roof-tops of other houses below, nearer the beach.

Mum, George and I stayed with the Cruse family for about two to three weeks whilst Ivy Cottage was being got ready for us, also our furniture had arrived in Bideford on the goods train from London, at a cost of £8 and Mr Stan Squires, the local carrier had brought it to Clovelly for us; all that remained now was for it to be brought down to the cottage. This was another eye-opener, for the local men agreed to bring it down for a few bob and they brought it down on sledges. My mum thought it so strange to see her sideboard lashed down with rope onto a sledges and see it slide under control down the High Street.

During this time we met many people in the village. Mr & Mrs Cruse introduced us to many villagers and Rachael introduced me to many of her friends, some of whom were evacuees from Peckham and Deptford who had come down at the same time as George. A special friend was Norah (Norrie) Lamey who lived with her family in a cottage called Temple Bar. Together with Norrie, Rachael and her sister I had many happy times in Clovelly.

We had a letter from dad to say that after waving us goodbye at the station, he had gone back and worked until the evening, when he had gone to his mother's. After having a meal there his mother had suggested that he stay the night instead of going back to an empty flat. The next morning, after a very heavy raid, he had gone back to the shop to start work and found the whole place a pile of rubble. He had already told the air-raid wardens that his wife and children had been evacuated and that only he would be living in the flat above the shop. So of course they were searching in the rubble for him. Everything, with the exception of some furniture sent down to us, had been destroyed. Everything that he and mum had worked for was now lost, just smashed pieces in the rubble. As the shop was his livelihood it meant that in addition to finding another home, he had to find work.

Eventually we moved into Ivy Cottage which was to be our home for some time. Conditions were pretty primitive to say the least. There was only one bedroom but we eventually had three single beds in it; mum and Ernie slept in one, George in another and me in the other one. This leads me to another incident and shows what a town girl I was. One night we were all fast asleep when I was woken up by a loud hissing sound that was coming from under my bedclothes. I called out to my mum and she wanted to know what it was in my bed. I told her that it was a creature that was hissing like a snake, and with that I jumped out of bed and climbed into bed with my mum and Ernie. What a terrible night's sleep we had, three of us in a single bed. The next morning we carefully pulled back the bedclothes on my bed and there sitting on the sheet, as bold as brass was the largest bumble bee you ever saw. My mum called me a few names you can be sure.

We had an open fire that could be switched over to heat the oven for cooking. We had to keep the kettle on the fire all the time for hot water. For a while there was no electricity, but as the workmen were installing it in a nearby house, my mum paid for it to be brought into Ivy Cottage, although it wasn't even our house, we wanted some of the conveniences we were used to.

As coal was rationed, there was not much of that about so it meant to keep the fire going, we had to scrounge or find wood. We soon learnt to walk the beaches and carry up any pieces of wood that had been washed ashore by the waves. Also, as we found our way around, we walked in the woods and collected any fallen wood from there and the woods stretched for miles, especially along the cliff-tops. Above the villages was a lovely private road that wound its way along the cliff-tops towards the main road. Each side of the road were hundreds of huge trees and as you walked along, you could look down on the smoking chimneys of the houses in Clovelly village. Mum and I often walked up there and came back loaded with wood, sometimes dragging branches behind us. At least it kept the fire going.

I remember on one occasion, the village seemed very quiet, quieter that usual, and on looking out of the window we couldn't see anyone. My mum, who never really settled down to the life in Clovelly, although she liked the people and appreciated all that some were doing for us, came away from the window and said, "Cor, this is a God-forsaken place, it's like a morgue". It was only afterwards that we discovered that a huge mine had washed ashore and was on the beach. The authorities had been called and the villagers living near to the beach had been evacuated. Somehow, we had been overlooked, but I doubt if we would have suffered anything more than blown-in windows if it had gone off.

Mr Stan Squires, who ran the carrier business between Clovelly and Bideford with his lorry, used to get certain bits of shopping for people who could not get into Bideford. One day my mum asked Mr Squires if he would get her a sack of potatoes and later that day he put them on our doorstep. A few minutes later, whilst my mum was outside looking at them, Mr Bert Braund walked by. He was the brother of our neighbour and knew us, so he called out, "Hello Mrs Cooper, how's your teddies ?" Well, my mum, what she called him. She thought he was being dirty or something and didn't know that teddies was the local dialect word for potatoes.

To help out with the family money, I got a job i the Red Lion Hotel inClovelly. It was only a short walk down the cobbles that took about two minutes. I used to start at 7-30 every morning for six days a week and I wouldn't be finished until about 9-30 or 10 in the evening. For that I got ten shillings a week. I know that when we were working hard in the kitchen, I used to tell the other girls that one day when I had sufficient money, I would come back and stay in the Red Lion with my husband for a holiday.

I remember on one occasion at the Red Lion, we were to expect about 150 soldiers for some sort of meal. Belle Whitefield, the landlord's daughter said that she would bake some rock cakes for them and the girls and ladies in the kitchen said, "God help them then if they eat them.". Well we served them their food and tea and presently there was such a noise coming from the dining room that I crept back and opened it slightly. What a sight! There they were, having the biggest 'bun-fight' you'd ever seen. They were throwing Belle's rock cakes at each other and the place was littered with them. It is a wonder that none of them got injured with being hit by one of the.cakes.

Quite a few well known public people came to live in Clovelly during this time and one I remember well was a famous radio personality named Nosmo King. He was on the radio on a regular weekly show and one of the things he did was monologues. I forget his real name now, but I remember he used to tell us that he got his stage name whilst sitting in a railway carriage one day. He looked up and saw the usual sign that said, "NO SMOKING" and split it up into Nosmo King. He was a very nice man and I think everyone in the village liked him and he would stop and talk to young and old.

On occasions my dad would get away from London for the week-end and come down to see us. Of course like most men, he found his way down to the Red Lion Hotel, on the quay and I remember him coming in after having a drink on his first visit, he said, "You'll never guess who I have been drinking with down at the pub?" and when we said, "Who", dad replied "Old Nosmo King, that fella that's always on the wireless, you know, monologues and that." Of course mum and I pretended to be surprised, but he saw through us and we had to tell him that we, like most people in the village, knew Nosmo King very well and that we all liked him. Nosmo King had a son, Jack Watson, who is now a very well known actor, and he used to come down to see his father. I remember him swimming and diving in from the top of the quay. He always looked a great big tough chap and he was very nice as well. Another personality who I remember coming down at about this time, was an actress named Betty Driver. Of course she is very well known as well.

I remember the time my mum was taken ill and the doctor was called. He came and decided that she had to go into hospital but as she couldn't walk she had to be carried up the street to meet the ambulance. Well, although my mum and I was worried how this was going to be done, the doctor and the locals were not bothered in the least. Soon there were a number of men at the door and they carried my mum up the street in a kind of sling that hung from two poles that the men put over their shoulders. There were sufficient of them to carry in relays and it transpired that this was the usual way of getting people that were ill, up to the ambulance. My mum and I often talked about that afterwards and I know she as so grateful for what they done. I remember that I couldn't go with her as I had to stay behind and look after the two boys.

My mum got more and more homesick for London, at least for Deptford and my dad. So after much discussion and agreement, she returned to London. My dad had found a furnished flat in the same area but the heavy daily bombing of the docks had stopped and he felt it was safe for her to come back. She got a job in a munitions factory whilst my dad continued work on bomb damage.

I had a new turn in my life, for I was to be a mother to my two small brothers, to look after them, to get them ready for school, cook their meals and tend to them when they were sick. I suppose it was more accepted in those days when the eldest girl in the family very often reared the younger ones so that mum could go out and earn some money for the family kitty. However I think a lot of people in Clovelly were surprised that I set about the job and if I do say it myself, I made a fair job of it. Whenever they could, mum and dad came down to see how we were and if I was coping all right. I mean, I was only about sixteen and I was bringing up my two younger brothers and managing the house. One time in the winter of 1941, they came down as far as Bideford but couldn't get any further because of eight-foot snow drifts prevented the buses from running.

Ernie hadn't started school yet but was getting into mischief whenever he could. Once after I had been out of the house for a few minutes, leaving him sitting quietly, I came back to find him playing with the clock. Now the clock wasn't mine, it had been lent to me by Norrie's mum and here was Ernie with the clock in his lap and he had broken off one of the hands. I was in a panic. What was I to do? I was frightened to go back to Mrs Lamey and say, "Sorry but my brother has just broken your clock." I sat down to think what I should do. Thinking wasn't easy with Ernie crying his head off because he knew he had caused some serious trouble for me. Then it came to me – that is if I could do it. I got a matchstick and shaped it a bit, then stuck it end ways over the stump of the broken bit of hand on the clock and then got some glue and stuck it properly. When it had dried, I darkened it with shoe polish and it went beautifully, but more about the clock later.

Living in a fishing village on a very rough bit of coast taught me about the necessity of having a lifeboat and how we should always help out whenever we could. If the lifeboat had to be launched at low-tide, it meant that there was no water on the slipway and that human muscle had to pull it across the pebbles to the sea. For this, nearly everyone turned out to help regardless of the weather. I used to run down to help and more than a few times I was in the water up to my chest as we all pulled to launch the boat. I remember that when I was in the water, the lifeboat used to appear as high as a mountain above me and then it was out to sea whilst we went back home to change and wait for their return. Since those days, I have had a lot of respect for the lifeboatmen who only seem to go out in very rough weather.

On one occasion after the lifeboat had been out some time, word was shouted around the village that the lifeboat was coming back in. Everyone ran down to the harbour as the boat came in and we saw that it was loaded with bodies of dead German airman. It was something that was apparently happening all the time, the German 'planes would attack either South Wales or the ships in the convoys off the coast, and the RAF fighters would come along and shoot down some of them.

The dog-fights between the German 'planes and our boys was something we often watched and if we were on top of the cliff, it seemed as if we were looking down on them and there are no prizes for guessing who we were cheering for.

As I was good with a needle, having been taught at school and at home, and in order to get some more money for myself, I asked my mum to send me down her old sewing machine. She agreed and eventually it arrived so I was able to let people know that I was ready to take in some sewing work. This was the time of rationing and coupons were necessary for all new clothes or material for dressmaking, but this didn't prove to be too much of a problem to me, as coming from a poor area of London, I knew about buying second-hand coats in good condition and then unpicking the seams and lining to provide 'new' clothes.

When people got to hear about this, I was inundated with work, the place always seemed to be full of pieces of cloth that was drying out after I had washed it. I used to iron the clean lining and material, sometimes turning it and remake the coat again or cutting it into a different garment.

I soon learnt that making money was one thing, spending it in Clovelly was another. Now, at this time I had never smoked in my life and I had often wondered what it was like so with my friends, Rachael and Norrie, I went into the Post Office in the High Street and bought a packet of twenty Kensitas cigarettes; they use to have a small packet attached on the side on the big one and which held just one cigarette with the words something like, 'one for your friend' written on the front. There was a picture of a butler with bow tie and tails holding a silver salver on which was a packet of Kensitas.

Anyway, I bought a packet and off we went and I had my first smoke. After a few puffs I started to feel ill and giddy, I suppose I was swallowing the smoke, I persevered, still feeling ill but thought it was normal and that it would go away, but it got worse and worse. I found I couldn't smoke anymore and then I was so ill I didn't want to see another cigarette. Oh I can still remember that horrible feeling of nausea and giddiness. There I was, nearly sixteen, smoking my first cigarette, when lots of kids had smoked before they had left school and I was vowing that I would never smoke again. I have kept that promise to myself and have never smoked again from that day onwards.

It was obvious that my mum and dad were worried about us as they were always writing and they sent my housekeeping money every week and I think I got a parcel every week from home. Rachael's Aunt Ruth used to deliver the post around the village and she used to say to Rachael, "My, that Rosie has some parcels, she has more than I've ever carried to anyone."

I remember the nice things as well as the hard and sometimes unhappy times that I spent as a child in Clovelly. The blackberry picking at the end of summer and coming home to make lots of blackberry jam for me and the boys. I had sufficient sugar as I used to save it from everyday use as none of us took it in our tea or cocoa. The boys loved blackberry jam on their bread and sometimes for a treat I would make the boys a cake but as dried fruit was rationed, there was never very many currants and sultanas in the cake. It was a case of 'hunt the currant'.

I could never get over the beauty of Clovelly; I suppose being a city girl I noticed it all the more and it made me realise how lovely the countryside was. Christmas time was especially lovely, although I might be homesick, the preparations for Christmas, getting things ready for the boys and decorating the cottage. The lovely greenery of the holly and the sprays of fir, then there were the fir cones that I used to collect and some of these I painted and either hung up or placed on the window sills. Although it was war time and people were being killed, Christmas still made us excited.

Some evenings I would go to Norrie's house and listen to the radio, mostly to Vera Lynn singing to the Forces. I loved to hear her sing but it made me so very very homesick and some of the songs reminded me of my old home in Deptford, a home now reduced to rubble and which I wouldn't see any more. I tried not to think of my home being a pile of bricks and wondered what the street looked like now. At the back of our old house in Deptford was the Royal Victorian Victualling Yard, which was something to do with the Royal Navy I believe and often we kids used to see the men coming out through the big gates on their way home from work. I hated the war and what it was doing for millions of people but it had brought me to Clovelly.

Clovelly Court, the manor house of the Hon.Mrs Betty Asquith, was turned into a convalescent home for wounded soldiers. I think part of it only was used by the Red Cross for this purpose and they were often in need of help to clean and carry, so I used to go up and help sometimes when I could. There was the occasion when they wanted blood donors and I volunteered to give some. I am still very petite and you can imagined what I was like in my early teens and they must have looked at me a bit strange when I said I would give some blood. Anyway, they said that as I was so small, they would only take three-quarters of a pint from me.

I didn't mind, but in the next bed, waiting his turn, was a huge sergeant from the army and he started taking the micky about me only going to give three-quarters of a pint of blood and he was shouting the odds about me to everyone. Well, when they came up to him to put the needle in, he just fainted. A great big strapping bloke who a few minute before was having a go at me, was now out cold. Well I had a good laugh at him and got a load more to join in. I had got my own back on him anyway and did he look silly.

I thought no more about this until a few days later, I was down by the water's edge with my friends when we suddenly saw him and a few of his mates coming our way. Before he reached us he was shouting that he was going to get his own back and he came at me. I went into the sea and he followed. I went deeper and he started to but when he got to a point where he would have to take his feet off the bottom, he stopped. I knew then that he couldn't swim so I stayed just out of his reach and gave him as good as he gave me. He had met a Deptford girl who wasn't going to take any of his rubbish and he went off, very mad and dripping wet. I never saw anything of him after that, so perhaps he was well enough to be sent back to his unit.

There was another group of soldiers that came to Clovelly, the Commandos. They were British and Canadian and as Clovelly was pretty well filled with evacuees and others, they billeted a lot of them in Hartland area and some of the farms and cottages in Higher Clovelly. They were a terrific bunch of boys and they were training for something special and were climbing the very high cliffs around Clovelly. I used to talk to one of them during his off duty times and discovered that his name was 'A.A. Clark' and that he came from Hackney in London; of course his mates nicknamed him 'Ack Ack' after the anti-aircraft guns. One day, unknown to the villagers, the commandos did a mock attack on the village and during the morning's housework I went out to empty some rubbish and there was Ack Ack crouched behind the dustbin. He gave me such a start, especially as he had his face all blackened and was in battle order. Another time he said he would meet me but he never turned up and I didn't think too much about it as I knew they were doing a lot of training and things were very strict. The next morning, I went outside to hang out some washing and saw someone on the Royal Navy boat waving flags, I watched him for a bit and thought nothing more than he was making a signal to the Coastguard. The next time I saw Ack Ack, he told me that it was him that was waving the flags and he was trying to tell me why he hadn't met me. I told him I was sorry but I couldn't read flag signals.

We were good friends and soon it came the time to say goodbye. He gave me a small leather bound dictionary, saying he thought it would come in handy for me as I wasn't very good at spelling. I still have that dictionary to this very day and my daughter is looking after it for me. After a few weeks they went off and we never saw them again but we heard later that they had taken part in the raid on Dieppe and that most of them were killed.

One day, I was in the cottage doing some cooking when the fire started to smoke like mad. It was billowing out across the room and even when I opened the windows and doors it was no better. Eventually, the boys and I had to get out of the house. Standing out on the Look-out were the usual bunch of local fishermen and they looked at me to see what was wrong. One of them Mr Jones, said, "What's wrong

George and Ernie Cooper on the seat at "Lookout" 1943

40

with thee Rose "and I said that the chimney was smoking and I didn't know how to stop it.

He told me that it was obvious that the chimney needed sweeping and the rest all agreed and when I asked where I could get hold of a sweep they all laughed. "No maid, you'll do it yo'self when we tell how to do it." Mr Jones then went on to tell me to go and cut a good bunch of holly and get some long sticks. I was to tie the sticks together and then tie the holly on the end. By poking the holly up the chimney and then raking it up and down I would clean the chimney. Well, I did what they told me to do, but as they hadn't told me about the mess I'd make, you can guess what state the cottage was in afterwards. Anyway, the chimney was clean and the fire burned well without smoking us out. I kept the contraption and occasionally used it again on the chimney.

Another crisis that I had to deal with at the cottage was when the loo was blocked. I got in touch with the Estate office and soon there was a knock on the door. On opening it, I saw that it was Bernard Abbott with his tool-bag over his shoulder. Now I knew Bernard and also knew that he had just left school to work as a carpenter for the estate and he must have thought that I needed some woodwork done. When I told him what the problem was, his face dropped. "Phew", he said, "my first day at work, it's a Monday morning and I have this job to do".

Talking about the loo in the cottage, I have to relate this story. The loo had a tiny window that looked out onto a lovely little cottage that was rented by some of the Bonham-Carter family, one of which was Mark. He would often be sitting on the little wall outside and more often than not, playing his flute. We would be sitting in our cottage when all of a sudden the loo would flush and when I looked out of the tiny window, there would be Mark, sitting on the wall playing his flute. We never really caught him playing the prank, but we strongly suspected him of reaching through the open tiny window and pulling the chain; in our minds he was the secret chain puller.

About this time, the Rectory coachhouse was converted into a canteen to give the evacuees a mid-day meal to help the rations of their foster parents. I was told that I could take George and Ernie up there and as I had made the journey, I offered to help serve the food. This became a regular thing and I remember George used to get extra from me because when it got to his turn, he used to give me a wink and I'd give him an extra baked potato or something. I'd be a liar if I said that I didn't get something to eat as well.

I remember the herring fishing time when the boats came in, sometimes loaded, and from our cottage you could see the fish glistening in the nets and boats. I never tired of that sight. It was so exciting and it also meant that we would have lots of cheap meals because there is nothing like a good Clovelly herring.

As any mother knows, looking after a very small child once they have found the use of their legs, is a full time job. One day I was busy cleaning or cooking in the cottage when I suddenly realised Ernie was missing. Quickly looking about I then rushed outside and just glimpsed a sight of him passing under Temple Bar, heading down towards the quay.

Shouting for George to stay in doors, I rushed down the winding street, slipping and sliding on the cobbles and by the time I had reached the bottom, there was Ernie playing in the water in the quay-pool. There always used to be water there, even when the tide was out, although not very deep thank goodness. It was deep enough for Ernie to paddle in up to his waist and start splashing as he laughed and chortled at the fun. With my arrival, his antics exaggerated until, still ignoring my instructions to come out, he fell over and thereby completely wetting himself all over. This frightened him and he started to bawl as he crawled out of the water to me and reaching dry land held up his arms for me to carry him. To get him home quickly and dry him off meant that I had to pick him up and carry him, so I was wet too.

As I struggled up the street, carrying a dripping wet Ernie, I thought that at least this experience would frighten him into keeping away from the water for a bit. How wrong I was; from now on I had to keep my eyes on him all the time if the front door was open. Once he got out, he'd be off down the cobbles to the quay-pool again and this happened time and again until he finally got fed up with his escape runs.

Another of my trials and tribulations as a young 'acting mum' was with George. One day I had dressed him up in his one and only best suit and sent him off along with some other children to go to Sunday School. A good while later, Rachael came to me and said that George was outside the cottage and wouldn't come in. I replied something to the effect to tell him not to be silly but to come in. It appeared that George was definitely not coming into the house as he was frightened over something. I went outside and saw George standing there looking all sorry for

Rose Cooper outside "Lookout Cottage" Clovelly. 1943

himself and then it suddenly hit me. The smell! I couldn't have him standing there like that, stinking the place out, what would people think. I dragged him inside and as I started to take his clothes off of him, he started to tell me what had happened.

On the way to church, the bunch of boys had decided to go instead to see if they could get some sea-gull eggs, which of course they had heard older boys and men talking about. Many local people ate them and I was told that they were all right as long as you didn't mind the fishy taste. Anyway, George and his mates had gone along the cliff edge and got quite a number of eggs, but being a city boy and a bit daft over such matters, he had collected some addled eggs as well as good one. They were all put into his jacket and trouser pockets and they made their return journey home. Of course boys being boys, they didn't walk home sedately and soon some of the eggs were broken in the pockets and it had to be the addled ones that broke. I don't think George will ever forget that episode in his life, as I nagged him continually that day and every time I washed his clothes, as I never seemed to get the smell out of them.

It was about this time that I discovered a large rat was living in the cottage with us; he used to come from the coal cupboard that was next to the fire in the kitchen. Some mornings, I would come out of the bedroom, down stairs and as I pushed the kitchen door open, I would see the rat sitting on one of the chairs, upright, in a begging position. I tried to catch it many times and always failed but as it didn't seem to bother us too much I eventually let it stay. Often I would see his tail protruding under the cupboard door. The rat stayed in the cottage all the time until we moved.

Another of my memories, like the herring fishing and the beautiful countryside, was that sometimes my friends and I would walk up from the village, through the lower part of Wrinkleberry Lane, past the school and then down along the main road (Slerra) back to the cobbles again. Continuing our walk, we would go right down to the bottom and sit on the quay; there we would sing all our favourite songs. In my mind, I can still hear our voices echoing up through the village, past the houses clinging to the side of the cliff.

With the war still continuing, my friends had reached the age where they were subject to call-up for National Service and they all went into nursing. That meant that I now had lost my usual friends and regardless of my work, my housekeeping and looking after two small boys, I was lonely.

From the news, it looked like the war with Germany would soon be over, at least there was no more bombing of London and it would be safe for me and the boys to return. My mum and dad had already been discussing this point with me and now that my friends were away, I agreed to return to London.

Notice was given to vacate the cottage and my mum and dad came down with my mum's brother to help with the move. Now, as you will remember, the furniture came down on sledges and the only problem was holding them back and steering. Now everything had to be carried up to the top of the cobbles so that Mr Squires could put it on his lorry to take it into Bideford for the train.

My uncle had never seen anything like Clovelly before and soon, after carrying heavy furniture up the street, he started to moan about what he was doing. To have him continue, my mum promised him a pint for every bit of furniture he carried up and this perked him up no end and soon he and I would be going up the street and when we reached the New Inn, halfway up, he would stop and disappear into the bar to have a pint whilst I minded the furniture in the middle of the street. When we came back down, empty handed, he knew it was no good stopping, he'd have to wait until we came up again. By the end of the long day, we had moved everything that we were taking back, with the exception of sufficient bedding and an old sofa that would remain.

I remember that night, because after we had all had a good meal, we lay down on the floor and covered ourselves with blankets. That is with the exception of my uncle, who was given the old sofa to sleep on. The next morning we all woke up early, as we knew we had a long day ahead of us, and as we were having a cup of tea my uncle said, "You will never guess what I have to tell you." He then went on to tell us that he had been been woken up in the night to find a large rat licking his toes that were sticking out from the blanket. Everyone laughed and I told him he must have been dreaming and neither the boys nor I let on about our rat in the coal cupboard.

After saying our goodbyes to various people, we left Clovelly. I had been in Ivy Cottage for four years.

There is a sequel to these memories. I have mentioned the fact that my little brother had broken the hand off the clock, and before we left Clovelly, I returned the clock to the Lameys, who had kindly lent it to me. I was too frightened to tell them about the mishap and my repair and this bothered me for years, When I returned to Clovelly with my husband John, I took with me a brand new clock and gave this to Norrie and then told her about the old one. I felt better after this.

CHAPTER FOUR

MY SISTER AND I

I don't suppose the name of Eileen Joyce King or my maiden name of Law, would ever have got into a book except for the war with Germany and my evacuation with lots of other children from my school, followed fifty years later by a re-union of many of those very same people.

I was born in Peckham in South London and at the outbreak of war I was attending Bellenden Road Elementary School, which was only a short walk from my home, 19, Avondale Rise, Peckham, from where my parents, Selina and Benjamin, carried on a business selling and delivering newspapers. Here I lived with my parents, brothers and sisters, and just after the war started in 1939 I was ten years old and my younger sister, Doreen, was not quite five. The rest of my brothers and sisters were older and the boys, who were in the printing trade, expected to be soon called up into the Services.

London was changing rapidly and already a lot of children had left our school to be evacuated to the countryside somewhere. Our teachers changed, as some were called up and others went away with groups of children. Our nearest park was Peckham Rye and this had been churned up with air-raid shelters and trenches being dug all over the lovely green spaces. Barrage balloons were already flying over London with the lorries they were attached to being stationed in all sorts of spare space. We children used to go and chat to the crews when the balloons were up and if we saw that they were being hauled down, we used to race to where the lorry and its crew were. Then we could see the winch pulling the balloon down and try to stand under the huge balloon. I remember the first time that I did this, I was surprised to see how large the balloon was.

We had our gas-masks from a fitting station in Bellenden Road, it was really a church hall and was used for this purpose. There were a lot of trestle tables with men behind them and on the tables were heaps of gas-masks. As people came up to the table, the men tried a gas-mask on them, adjusting the straps if necessary until it was a fairly good fit. Instructions were given on how to keep it clean and stop the condensation building up on the eyepiece. Small children got a different type and little babies had something like a closed-in carry cot with a large window on the top and with a pump on the side for the parents to ensure that sufficient air was provided for the child.

In the Spring of 1940, my father suffered a stroke and was taken to hospital; and this coupled with the worry of trying to keep the business running in difficult times, and her concern about my my sister and I; was enough for my mother to decide that her two youngest should be evacuated out of London.

There was one problem, the official evacuation was restricted to school children, and Doreen had not started at school and would not be five until the 15 July. My mother had told the school that if Doreen could not go, then she would not let me go; definitely not on my own. After some discussion by the authorities, common sense prevailed, and Doreen was allowed to be evacuated – as long as I went with her.

On 14 June 1940, it was a fine sunny morning, and although fairly early it was already getting hot, when we marched out of Bellenden Road School with our gas-masks slung around our shoulders in the brown cardboard boxes that came with it, and carrying our cases, packs or parcels of belongings. Every child had a label tied to a coat, shirt or blouse and on it had the child's name and address, age and the name of the school.

Doreen Law, Mrs. Nell Beer, Eileen Law. 1940

Along Bellenden Road we marched, in the centre of the road, then right, into Blenheim Grove to the Peckham Rye railway station. There were lots of parents, relatives and interested people walking along on the pavement, shouting messages to the children and shouts from the children in reply. Some children started to sing a song or two, just like the army. For many it was a great adventure, for other a frightening time.

My mother had said her good byes at home and did not come to the school or the station. She was a very private person and I suppose if she wanted to have a weep, she would do it quietly at home or in the shop. I know that when she gave us the last cuddle and kiss before we left, she was very upset and I discovered later that she nearly changed her mind at the last minute about us going away.

There was a train waiting for us in the station, we boarded it and off we went. I do not remember much about the journey, we had some teachers with us as well as escorts and they had their hands full trying to cope with a train load of children. They seemed for ever going up and down the corridors to check on the children in the separate compartments, it was not like the open railway carriages of today. At some stage of the journey, the train stopped in a large station and there were lots of tables loaded with cakes, sandwiches and such like for the children. There were lots of ladies with white aprons waiting on us and everyone was very friendly to us. Having been fed, the train went on again until it stopped at Bideford in North Devon.

When we got off the train we were split into various groups and my group walked around the corner from the station and into a church hall or something. Here we were washed and they inspected our hair. After that we were given more food until the time came for us to move again, this time on buses, and Doreen and I climbed up the stairs to travel on the top, so that we could see the countryside. We asked an adult where we were going and they said, "Clovelly, which is in North Devon." Well it meant nothing to us children. I remember when someone first saw the sea and everyone rushed to the right-hand side of the bus to see. There were screams of delight from some – we were going to the seaside. The buses took us to Clovelly Court, the manor house of the village, which is about ten miles from Bideford and there was a large crowd of ladies to meet us as we got off the bus.

Standing there on the grass with little Doreen, and she was small for her age, with our belongings beside us, I felt a surge of nervousness, but I couldn't let her see that I was, else she might have started to cry. I was the older sister and as far as she was concerned, nearly grown up.

The ladies started coming along the lines of the children, looking at them, reading the details on their labels and occasionally asking questions. One lady wanted me but not my sister, "Oh, she's too small." she said, "She will always be crying for her mother."

Then a younger lady came up and she called out, "Auntie, come here, here's two nice little girls." An older lady came over to us and I could see that she was not too happy with Doreen, as I have said, she was very small for her age. There was some discussion between the two ladies and it was agreed that we should go with them. We had been selected.

Up the hill we walked for about half a mile, to a cottage which was on the main road at a part called Slerra Hill. In the cottage was the older lady's husband and he was all smiles and oozing friendship. The couple's names were Arthur and Nell Beer and the younger lady was Nell Beer's niece, Maggie. Mr Beer said that he had stood outside the cottage and saw the buses going past, on their way to Clovelly Court and had seen Doreen standing up in the front on the upper deck of the bus, and he had thought, "That's a pretty little maid, I wouldn't mind taking in that one," and now here she was.

We settled in quickly into a very friendly home. We had written to my parents to tell them where we were and that it was nice. Gradually, got used to the country way of life. It was strange to start with, no water in the house, no electricity and the toilet was up the garden. We started to call Mr and Mrs Beer, 'Uncle' and 'Auntie' and they accepted it. We discovered that most of the evacuees addressed their foster parents as Auntie or Uncle, although one used the term Grannie and Granfer. If there was not much warmth in the relationship between evacuee and the foster parents, then the term was always a polite Mr and Mrs or Miss.

For some reason or other the local school was not ready for the evacuees; I don't know whether they did not want to take us in, or as there were so many London children, perhaps there just was not enough room to fit us all in. I discovered that in addition to Bellenden Road school, there was similar group of children from Evelyn Road school in Deptford, and that made a total of over one hundred and fifty, I believe. To keep us under some sort of discipline, we used to meet our teachers at various places and then go off with them. The London teachers that came down with us were Mr Bamsey, and Miss Plaice from Peckham and Miss Woods from Deptford. We would go off for nature walks through the lanes, fields and woods. Sometimes we would go to the beach, either at Clovelly or to the next village along the coast – Bucks Mills. The teachers were very good and between them and our foster parents, those of us who wanted to, learnt a lot about the flowers and the trees.

I shall never forget my first visit to Clovelly village, what a lovely sight it was when I went down the cobbled street. I remember that as we went down the High Street with Auntie Nell, Doreen and I were amazed at the houses perched on the side of the cliff along each side of the High Street. Most of the houses had their front doors open and there were masses of flowers in pots and window boxes outside every house. Looking into the hallways of the houses you could see lots of gleaming brass and shiny floors. It seemed that everyone knew Auntie and there were words and smiles for Doreen and I. It seemed a friendly place in those days.

Later on in life I came to know that Clovelly is unique in itself, having a steep cobbled High Street, where no motor vehicles are allowed, and it is doubtful whether many would be able to negotiate the street other than the first part which is without steps. As it is for pedestrians only it makes it more enjoyable to walk down without the fear of traffic. Coming up is a different matter, especially for the middle-aged and elderly, but with frequent stops along the way, they all make it. As Clovelly is so famous, visitors come from all over the world to see it and the donkeys, which are associated with it. The donkeys have always been used for bringing down goods for the shops and beer for the New Inn Hotel, which is half way down the High Street. They were also used to carry up the rubbish and empties from the village. At one time they were also used to carry up visitors who could or would not face the long climb. . At the bottom of the High Street is a little harbour with lots of fishing boats.

In 1940, even with some of the fishermen already in the Forces, Clovelly had more boats than the present day and the fishermen were from families that had lived and worked in Clovelly for generations. When the teachers took us down into Clovelly village we learnt about the sea and sea creatures and fishing from the fishermen. We would watch the fishermen at work cleaning and painting their boats, mending their nets whilst they sat on the quay and if you peeped into one or two of the old sheds you could sometimes see them making their lobster pots from willow cane.

The fishermen had marvellous patience with the children, explaining how different fish were caught at certain times of the year, like seasons. Answering the hundred and one questions from eager and excited London children, who in their moments of not feeling homesick, regarded it as a great adventure. I loved sitting on the quay and listening to them, even though I had not as yet, had a full understanding of the local dialect and there were many words that I did not comprehend. No doubt the fishermen was just as puzzled over our accent, especially as the south London accent was not exactly King's English. The fishermen liked telling us stories from their life on the sea, and many of them had served apprenticeships in three-masted sailing boats trading around the world, one told us that he had sailed away from home on a three-master at the age of twelve years.

Another attraction for us children in the village was the lifeboat and the lifeboat house, with its slipway jutting across the beach to the sea. We liked to go inside and gaze up at the boat, all beautifully painted in blue and white with bits of red. Then all the equipment hanging on the wall and the board showing all the ships that the lifeboat had gone out to. This was all new to us and it reminded me of the stories about Grace Darling and her father that I had read about.

Raymond Lamb; Charlie Beaumont Betty Cook; Eileen Law;
Phyllis Cook; Ken Cook; Roy Cook

We often went down to the village, not all the way down but as far as Mount Pleasant, where uncle's brother Ernest lived. He was deaf and dumb and a very nice kind man liked by most people. He had been trained as a tailor, having gone away to London or somewhere to learn the trade and this had been paid for by Mrs Christine Hamlyn, the aunt of Mrs Betty Asquith, and who until 1936, was the owner of Clovelly. Although he still did a bit of tailoring during the war, he worked mostly with the donkeys. I liked to go and visit him and his sister and brother-in-law, with whom he lived and their home was just like auntie and uncle's. The kindness must have run in the Beer family, they were all so nice.

As the summer of 1940 was so beautiful, we had plenty of nature walks and stories. On the occasional wet day we would go into a barn and have our lessons there. Mr Bamsey or Miss Plaice were very good with us and taught us how to spell and do mental arithmetic, as well as teaching us about nature. As we had no books to read from or to write in, it was important that we continue with our studies some way and we were always being urged to read whatever books or newspapers we could find in our foster homes. Most of the books were old Victorian type novels with long hard words, but it got us to read and most of the tales were interesting.

By the end of the summer, Doreen and I were well and truly settled in with Mr and Mrs Beer and it was strange how they took sides

Eileen Law, Phyllis Cook and Doreen Law outside No. 115 Slerra Background: Mary and Peter Littlejohns, Mrs Littlejohns, Mrs. D. Cook. 1940

with us. Uncle always took Doreen's side in a dispute between us but Auntie would say, "Oh she's not so innocent Arthur, Doreen can be just as naughty." I think Uncle thought that as I was the eldest, I should give way in every argument but sometimes I didn't feel that I should.

It was a lovely home that they gave us, Auntie always made sure that we had a good breakfast before we left in the mornings and later on, when the Old Rectory coach-house was opened as a canteen for the evacuee's lunches, we had our mid-day meal there and when Uncle came home in the evening, we had another cooked meal with him. Although it was war-time with rationing, Auntie always seemed to have enough to make good meals for us all, she was a wonderful cook and made such lovely pasties and cakes, I am amazed that she made so much with so little. Some of the things she made, make my mouth water even now, there were potato and cream pasties, parsley and egg pasties, leek pie and 'raw teddy fry', which is potato and onions fried in a pan with bacon. It is very tasty and I often cook it now. When the herrings were in season, auntie would cook them several ways and they were all scrumptious. Other things she made were of course, cakes and sponges, fruit tarts, jam puddings, brawn and pigs trotters. She seemed to make something out of nothing and I suppose she had to with four of us to feed and I was always hungry, so she had an never ending task.

Mr Theo Beer or his brother Tommy, who were bakers, delivered bread in their little van to Clovelly twice a week. They were cousins of uncle and they lived and worked in Hartland. Another cousin of uncle was Mr Bill Beer of Crossland Farm, Higher Clovelly, which was only 100 yards up the road from us. He delivered the milk with his yoke across his shoulders holding two big buckets with lids. He came very early in the mornings and Auntie would go to the door with her jug and Mr Beer would pour out a measure and probably there would be a covered cup of clotted cream as well. Sometimes he had his evacuee with him, Harry Clement from Peckham, who I had known for some time, as we used to share a desk in Bellenden Road school. Mr Jim Cruse or his daughter Joan, delivered meat in their van twice a week and there was a grocer who called, as well as Mr Hubert Jeffrey from Hartland selling coats, trousers, breeches, shirts and socks, as well as clothes for the ladies. Clovelly had a carrier, Mr Stan (Yangy) Squires, who had a lorry and he made daily trips into Bideford, taking and fetching goods. He would even do some shopping for people if you gave him the instructions and you paid him when he got back. He was a wonderful help to most people.

Although I used to write home often and tell everyone how happy we were with Auntie and Uncle, I suppose until they had seen where we were living or how we looked, they would not be happy. That first summer saw the visits by some of my older brothers and sisters, particularly Violet, who came as often as she could. Generally, we all had a good time, considering they were only short brief visits. Doreen and I would be taken into Bideford on the bus and buy us lunch or tea, take us shopping where they would buy things for us, as well as things for themselves which they couldn't get in London. I seem to remember that two of the favourite places were Heywood & Cocks and Mr Goodenough. They would usually buy our shoes from Mr Goodenough and as he used to travel out to the villages in his little car, if anything needed doing to the shoes later on, he would collect them and take them back to his shop. During these visits from the family, the trip to Bideford usually ended with going to the cinema (pictures) and then after having a very happy day out, back onto the bus and back to Auntie's.

One of my local friends was Phyllis Cook, who lived next door to Auntie and Uncle's cottage. Her's was a large family, some grown up whilst about five were still at school. Phyllis and her sister Betty, although she was often ill with asthma, used to take Doreen and I out on walks at week-ends and they showed us the wild strawberries and the nuts and berries they we could eat. We used to pick leaves and flowers and I would take them home to dry, so that I learnt about them. They took us down to the Hobby Drive, which is a road through the woods at the top of the cobbles and snaked around the top of the cliffs until it comes out on the main road to Bideford. The road crosses a few streams running down the hillside and as you walk along, you can look down on the roofs of the village and then out across the bay towards Westward Ho!

Other friends that I had close to me were Ken and Roy Cook, who were Phyllis's brothers, Ron and Pat Lomas, evacuees from Peckham, Mary Littlejohns who lived in Slerra Hill Farm, although she, like Harry Clement, did not come out to play very much as they were working on the farm after school. There was also Raymond Lamb, from Peckham, Gloria and John Pillman staying with their grandparents, Grampie Squires, for the duration, Donald Evans from Bristol and living with Uncle Jim Bragg,

Margaret Bragg and her sister Greta, George Smith and Norman Headon. There were three Deptford evacuee girls living with Mrs Irene Headon in Slerra, but she would not let them come out to play with the rest of us, they could only mix with us at school. They were nice girls and very unhappy about their restrictions.

In the autumn, it was lovely to walk along the Hobby, with the leaves all changing colour and to gather the horse-chestnuts (conkers). We used to come back loaded with them and then sit in doors, making holes in them with a skewer so we could thread a piece of string through them to play conkers. It was mainly a boys' game but many of the girls played it as well and I soon learnt how to avoid getting my knuckles rapped when taking a swing at someone else's conker. There were some beautiful sweet chestnut trees in Clovelly and each autumn we would go and pick as many as we could find, then take them home and keep them in the dark until Christmas. We would do the same with hazelnuts which we picked from the hedges.

Another practical task that I could do when enjoying my walks was to pick up any fallen wood from the trees, or to pick up the wood chips from where a tree had been cut with an axe. I would bring these home to Auntie in a bag and they would be put to one side to dry and later used in the cooking stove. Before winter came, Uncle would have a great big pile of wood stacked up ready beside the shed and this would be gradually used throughout the winter for heating, cooking and for hot water. Thankfully, there was always plenty of wood about and the local people, who were tenants of the Clovelly Estate, were allowed to pick up wood from beneath the trees, or what was left after the tree fellers had carted a big tree away.

We started school before the cold wet weather came and when we were first shown into the little school at Wrinkleberry, most of us that had been used to the big schools in London, could hardly believe that it really was a school. To accommodate all the children, and there were about one hundred and fifty evacuees as well as thirty-odd local children, into three classrooms, they had divided the big room (the hall) into four spaces by hanging curtains across on wires. This now gave them room for six class and even though there were not enough desks to go around, we started our education again. One of the big problems with having classroom walls made of thin curtains was that you could always hear the teachers in the classes each side of you as you were having a lesson. Just when you started to think and work out an arithmetic question, one of the classes would start having dictation or reading.

At first, although we knew some of the local children by this time, there was some understandable friction between the two groups. They had been very happy until we arrived and forced them into the squashed-up situation and they had not only to give up their school space, but some of their books as well. Instead of having a reading or text book for every child, it became normal for the books to be shared between two or three children. There was a shortage of pencils, so many had to make do with slates to write on. There seemed to be a great misunderstanding amongst local people as to where Cockneys came from. We were all dubbed cockneys, even though we were not. To tell the Clovelly people that we came from Peckham or Deptford in south London meant nothing to them, to them, all Londoners were Cockneys.

If we had been in London in normal times, I would have been sitting my examination for the grammar school (11-plus). I don't know what happened, but none of the London children I knew, sat any examination at Clovelly in 1940/41. Perhaps it was because of the war, or maybe the fact that we had just lost a year of our schooling. It was in this state that our schooling staggered on towards Christmas 1940.

That first Christmas was an experience, because Uncle took us down to the woods and we chose our very own Christmas tree. Carrying it back up the hill was hard work for Uncle, whilst Doreen and I carried the holly. With the long winter evenings, sitting in the kitchen with a good fire going was a lovely experience for two London children. There was no electricity so lighting was by oil lamps and Auntie would light one after we came home from school and put it on the table. It had a warm yellowish glow, not as bright as an electric light, but it seemed nicer. If we were not talking, or listening to the radio, I would sit at the table and read or write letters home or to my brothers and sisters. Also to my mother and occasionally to my father, who was seriously ill, having had a stroke earlier and who was now in a hospital in Stoke-on-Trent, his London hospital having been evacuated.

Not long after we came to Clovelly, I had been told that my brother Albert was missing in action in the fighting in France. Apparently he had landed at Calais with his regiment, the Green Jackets on the 22nd May and it was sometime before my parents were told that he was a prisoner of war. We learnt later that he was captured on the 26th May, just five days after landing at Calais. Then I got my first card from him from the prison camp, Stalag VIIIB. I was so excited; he did not have much room to say a lot and of course it was written in pencil. Although he was allowed only a few cards a month write to all the different members of the family, he still managed to write to Doreen and I. Regularly throughout the war he wrote, and as I used to write back to him and send him photographs of Doreen and I,, he would comment on how we had grown. On Saturday nights, my treat was to listen to 'In Town Tonight 'on the radio. Every week, when the announcer used to say after the signature tune, "Carry-on London." I felt so proud, although I wasn't very old.

In the winter evenings, when it got to the time for Doreen and I to go to bed, Auntie would make us a cup of cocoa, give us a sweet each and then carrying a candle to see the way, we would go off up to bed. I have often thought about those sweets that Auntie used to give us, as they were more than our own sweet ration, we must have been taking their's.

Being a town girl, I was anxious to see as much as I could on a farm and in Clovelly, in those days, there were a lot of farms, much smaller than today, but enough to give people a living then. One of the farms just down the road from Auntie's was one that was farmed by Mr and Mrs Bragg. He was a nice old man, white hair and moustache, she was a tall lady and had been a schoolteacher at Wrinkleberry, there was one son, Edgar and he was in the army. Uncle Jim Bragg, as we children called him, let us help him on the farm, doing small jobs, once he had shown us how to do it. I went down to his farm as often as I could to help feed the pigs, calves and chickens. I was helping him and I was learning about the country at the same time. When corn harvest came around, he like many farmers, was glad for any help he could get. Some Saturdays we would take the horse and cart to some of his fields out on the Bude road and then we would dig potatoes, bag them, load them and bring them back to the barn in Clovelly. I loved going there, because he would always let me drive the horse when we came off the main road into the lane that led to the fields. He would just hand me the reins and say, "Go on, get on with it maid."

There was another farmer who had a few acres and some livestock who allowed me to go and feed his chickens and calves. He, Grampie Squires, taught me how to feed a calf by putting my hand in a bucket of milk and letting the calf suck my finger and take in the milk. Sometimes he would let me collect the eggs. Often I would walk with him across the footpath from Slerra to his son's farm at Hugglepit. His son Tommy was the tenant of a large farm and he had lots of cows and horses and several exciting barns to explore. Once I walked with Grampie Squires all the way to the village of Woolsery, which is about three miles, driving a cow and baby calf to the monthly auction. I remember they fetched £20

That first winter in Clovelly was our initiation of what a hard winter in the countryside could be like. Very deep snow and everywhere frozen up. No buses, (we only had two each day to Bideford) and no timber lorries, carrying the trees up from the woods for the war effort. Although I had been used to deep snow in Peckham and the winter of 1939 had been a very hard one there, it seemed so much more out in Clovelly. Mr Cruse, the butcher used to deliver meat to the houses in his little van but I don't remember how he managed in the snow, maybe he walked. The two bakers that normally made twice weekly visits to Clovelly from the next village at Hartland, did not come through the snow in their vans and although it was a day or so late, I seem to remember us always getting our bread.

Just down the road from Auntie's was a farm called Boathouse Farm, tenanted by Mr and Mrs Dick Headon and their son and daughter-in-law. They had a lodger who had just come down from London, named Mr Watson and he was a stage and radio personality by the name of 'Nosmo King'. He was a very nice man and everyone appeared to like him and he was friendly with all of us. Sometimes he would say to us, "Listen to 'In Town Tonight' on Saturday, I'm going to be on that programme." He used to do monologues and things and was very enjoyable. Mr Watson's son, Jack, used to come down and visit him and of course he is now a very famous actor. Every time I see him in a film on TV. my mind goes back to those war-time days.

In February 1941, about fifty evacuee children came to Clovelly from Bristol because of the bombing there and in May about the same number came from Plymouth which was being hit very hard at the time. All these had to be squeezed into our school somehow.

On Sundays, after breakfast, Doreen and I would go to Sunday school in the canteen or the Rectory. The Rector was the Rev. Cavendish and his children were usually away at boarding school. After Sunday school it was across the road to All Saints' church for Matins, as I sang in the choir. Mr Tom Finch was the organist and choir master and either George Smith a local boy or Ray Lamb, an evacuee from

Peckham, worked the hand-pump for the organ from a little seat, tucked away out of sight at the side of the organ.

On Sunday evenings I sometimes went to the Methodist chapel with my friends, Phyllis and Betty Cook and Mary Littlejohns. The chapel was quite a walk from Slerra, about one and a half to two miles each way, out on the Hartland road and if the weather was not nice, it could be a dreary journey. One thing was though, there were usually boys at the chapel in the evening and afterwards we would all walk back together, talking and gaming around; it was all part of going out on a Sunday evening.

Uncle was a bell-ringer at All Saints Church Clovelly but owing to the government ban on church bells being rung unless there was a German invasion, he was saved that journey every Sunday. He was also an Air-raid Warden being responsible for part of Higher Clovelly, that is the houses and farms alongside the main road leading to the village. Before the war he had been a member of the Rocket Apparatus Cliff Rescue Team for the Clovelly district. That was rescuing sailors from their ships after they had gone aground on the rocks near to the coast. I think they fired rockets at and over the ship with ropes attached and then brought the crew off the sinking ship by means of a seat being pulled on the line.

We children had to do our bit for the war effort, the boys used to dig for victory in the two gardens that were given to the school and we all used to sit in the playground on fine days and make huge camouflage nets for the army, we all went

Girls' Dancing Class outside The Stables at Clovelly Court.
Front row: Phyllis and Betty Cook; second Row: Eileen Law (centre). 1941

around the area, even to outlying farms, collecting metal, rags and paper salvage, bringing it back to school in barrows, old prams and even on sledges in the winter. We girls had cookery lessons from Mrs Hilton, the Estate Manager's wife, at East Dyke Farm and we also helped out sometimes in the old Rectory canteen. The cook in charge, Mrs Thorpe, was lovely. We called her 'Cookie', which she liked and she taught us a lot of things in cooking. We helped with the lunches and the clearing up afterwards and she always had a good word for me, saying that I was a good worker. We spent so much time out of school doing all these things that once again, because of the war, our education was suffering.

My other brothers were now in the army, Laurie was a Gunner in North Africa, Percy was in the Horse Guards, and Ben was in the Airborne and later fought in France and Germany. Laurie was like a father to Doreen and I, in fact after dad's illness, he more or less took over and always made sure that there was enough money to buy clothes for us. Before he went abroad, he left sufficient money with one of my sisters to buy us clothes when we needed them. I still have all the letters they wrote to me, even the prisoner of war cards, and they have given me all the letters I wrote to them during the war. I used to go out Carol singing with other children to raise money to give to the Red Cross for 'War Parcels'. I remember they cost fifteen shillings each and I thought that by raising that amount of money, a parcel would go out to Albert in his prisoner of war camp.

The lady who owned Clovelly was Mrs Betty Asquith who lived in Clovelly Court, which was a fine big manor house with magnificent views over the bay and out to Lundy Island. She was very kind to the children and arranged lots of parties and socials for us. At Christmas, there was a lovely tea party in Long Passage in Clovelly Court and a present for every child. Afterwards we would have games, which were organised by her and her friends and she always seemed to enjoy it as much as us. Because of the war, she had her sister, Mrs Angela Ruthven come to stay at the cottage at Mouth Mill, a little rocky bay within the parish. Somehow or other they decided that I would make a 'nice girl' to help out in the cottage during the holidays and week-ends and Mrs Asquith wrote a note to me asking that I call down to the Court to see them. I was now just over twelve and a call from Mrs Asquith was like receiving a summons from the Queen nowadays and so off I went to see them.

I got the job and the arrangements were that I collect a bicycle from the stables and ride through the woods to Mouth Mill. So on my first morning I walked down the hill to Court stables, got the bike and rode to Mouth Mill along the rough track that serves as a road. After I had finished all the work I rode back, more up hill this time, and left the bike at the stables and then walked up the steep hill to Aunties cottage in Slerra. I can't say it was an easy job, especially for a twelve year old, but the money was handy and the journey downwards was great, as going along quietly, I would see all kinds of wildlife, often I would see deer on each side of the road in the woods. Mrs Ruthven had two daughters and one was interested in collecting butterflies, so we would go out together, although I was not really a friend, perhaps their mother sent me out with them to keep them company.

In between doing other things, I went down the road to Mr Bragg and helped his wife Ellen, with her housework. She taught me to make butter in the old fashioned way and if the weather was warm, we used to go outside and put cold water in to cool the butter down, as there were no such things as refrigerators in the houses and farms in Clovelly in those days.

I once entered a flower competition at school and I won. I had collected over 100 different ones and I knew the common names of them all. Mr Hesketh did not believe me and so he tested me, just to satisfy himself, although that was not part of the competition. Considering that we had no books on botany, I think that I did well for a small London child. My prize was a Savings Stamp for one shilling or it may have been for two shillings.

Mr Hesketh introduced the game of shinty to the children and we used to play on the Lawn at Clovelly Court or on the cinders of the Upper Car Park. There were boys teams and girls teams and we used to enjoy ourselves but no doubt because it was unknown or unpopular in other villages around, we never got to play other schools. A Plymouth teacher, Miss Pam Williams, took the girls for sport and we had some good shinty players among the girls, Mary Littlejohns, Betty Newman, Pat Richards, and Rosemary Buckingham from Plymouth. I liked sport and would often go down to the harbour with the other children to swim, but I was never very good although Doreen became a super swimmer after a while. When we had first gone to the beach, she would scream and shout every time I got her near to the water. There was the occasion when whilst out swimming not far from the beach, I suddenly got cramp and started going under. Two of the fishermen nearby, came in and got me out of the water. We girls used to go into the lime-kiln so that we were out of sight when we got changed.

Although I liked Mr Hesketh when he was out playing sport with us, there were times when I did not like him in the school. I remember the time when he caned me. As I have said, books in school were scarce and as far as the writing books were concerned, these had to be filled right up, with writing on the inside and outside of the covers before a new book could be issued. I believe there was only about one and a half books per pupil each year, so we wrote on all sorts of stuff. The day in question he shouted out, "Laws!" I went out to his table and he had my writing book in his hand. "Why have you torn a page out of your book?" I must have gone very red in the face and I stammered, "I haven't sir." He opened the book, turning the blank pages until he came to where there was a loose sheet, he pulled it out and it came away easily and it had torn edges on one side. Standing up he took his cane from the table, "Hold out your hand, the next time you are asked a question tell the truth." With that he caned me on both my hands in front of the children, not only in my class but in the other classes in the curtained off areas as well. This lesson, that he taught well, has served me satisfactorily through my life.

Blackberry time was a favourite with me, when we would go out with our baskets and fill them up with lovely juicy fruit. Auntie made, and she taught me as well, blackberry and apple jam and blackberry and apple pies, it was lovely with cream. Sometimes we would go miles seemingly, to pick the best and I remember once going with Mary Littlejohns out to the moors on the Bude road. There were huge blackberry bushes you could walk around with the biggest berries you could wish for. Whilst there, I happened to look down and saw near to where I was standing, an adder (they were called vipers)in the dry grass. I shouted to Mary and we were out of that moor and over the gate without a second thought about the lovely blackberries we were missing.

Two ladies had come to live in Clovelly for the duration of the war, one was Miss Woodall, who I was given to understand was a relation of the Cadbury family, and her friend, Miss Scott. They were both very nice ladies and they started a dancing school for the girls and somehow they made arrangements with Mrs Asquith to use one of her properties. The dancing classes were on a Saturday morning and we danced and skipped to music. It was mainly evacuee girls that took part, although Phyllis Cook and one or two other local girls came along. Both ladies took lots of group photographs of the girls and they were usually taken outside the stables.

Both ladies were very good teachers, although usually it was Miss Scott that did the teaching and Miss Woodall who operated the gramophone. I remember one tune that was a favourite of us all and that was 'Blaze Away'. After a while they decided that we were good enough to dance in front of an audience and we put on a show, but I don't know whether or not it was in conjuction with others and that we were just another act. Both ladies were kind and on my twelfth birthday, Miss Woodall bought me a present of the Book of Common Prayer. I still have it, and the paper it was wrapped in as I treasure it so much.

Auntie, like most people in Clovelly, had to fetch all of her drinking water from either a tap or a pump which would be at the side of the road and could be up to one hundred yards away from the house. Uncle used to carry at lot into the house when he came home from work and as we got older, both Doreen and I helped as well. For the washing water, auntie had large rain barrels, both front and rear of the house. We would also wash in rainwater and our baths were normally taken in front of the fire in the kitchen, after the water had been heated on the fire.

Just up the road from our house was the blacksmith. There was Mr and Mrs Bob Gist, their son Leonard and his wife and another son, Bill. I loved to go up and stand in the open doorway and watch them do the shoeing, the sparks from the iron as the hammer hit it and the fire. One thing though, I did not like the smell of burning hoof. We used to go each week to Mr Gist to have the radio accumulator charged and they also sold paraffin for the oil lamps we had in the houses. There was a shop in Higher Clovelly, in Shop Lane just off from Turn Pike. Mr Cook sold all sorts of things from flour to aspirin, sticking plaster to dates. Although there was a visiting grocer, most people in Higher Clovelly were registered for their rations with Mr Cook.

As the war went on, so children started to drift back to their homes in the cities for various reasons. This gave us a bit more space in the school but we had to say goodbye to some who we had made friends with.

By the time we came to break up from school for the Christmas holidays in 1943, I was fourteen and at the break I left school. I had already decided that I wanted to stay in the area and on 3 February 1944 I started work at Pilmouth Farm, near Bideford.

Doreen stayed on with Auntie and did not return to London until 1945 when the remainder of the children went back. I went back to London for two weeks holiday just before Doreen returned, so that I could settle her in at home.

Betty and Jill Gadd in Burscott Lane, Clovelly. 1940

When I arrived at Waterloo railway Station, I was worried my mother would not recognise me, as the last time she had seen me, I was only ten and now I was a teenager and grown up with lipstick on... I saw her at once, but she couldn't believe it was me, she kept saying, "But you're a young lady now, where's my little girl gone to?"

Both mum and I went to the station to meet Doreen when the time came for her return. Again, mother could not believe this was her daughter. Doreen had left home at four years of age and here she was nearly eleven. Such a long time to miss someone growing up.

After two weeks in London and seeing Doreen settled in back at home again, I returned to Devon. I was glad to be back, London appeared to be all bomb damaged, dirty and noisy and I yearned for the peace and quiet of the farm. Later on in life, I married a local man and I still live in the area

CHAPTER FIVE

FIVE DIFFERENT BILLETS

It was my brother Jack's second birthday on the 14 June 1940, when my sister Betty and I marched with a crowd of other children from our school, Bellenden Road School, in Peckham, South London to the local railway station. We marched down the middle of the road like soldiers, in ranks and some of the children were singing what they thought were military marching songs, one being 'Roll out the barrel', in which I joined until my aunt, who was acting as an escort, told me not to sing it; it being considered 'not a nice song for children to sing'. I remember the blue sky that morning and when I looked up, it appeared as if the sky was full of barrage balloons.

We were all about to be evacuated from London to the countryside, and neither child nor parents were aware of our destination. For many of us, carrying case, pack or parcel of belongings, with our gas-mask containers slung around our shoulders,, this was a great adventure. For the more sorrowful ones being comforted by older children or teachers, this was a great calamity. Each child had a large paper label attached to his or her coat on which was written the child's name, address and school. Mine read, Jill Gadd, 34, Maxted Road, Peckham, London, S.E.15; Bellenden Road Infants School.

Until that morning, I lived with my parents (Ida and Dick Gadd) and my brother and sister in a house in Maxted Road, just around the corner from the school, and I remember that life was comfortable and gentle, that there were plenty of green spaces for us to play in, Goose Green was just up the road from where I lived; Peckham Rye Common and Park, Dulwich Park and One Tree Hill were all within walking distance. And then Hitler came along and spoilt it all for us.

Even as a five year old child, one just couldn't fail to notice that something terrible might be on the horizon and that something was worrying my parents. Strange objects called barrage balloons were being flown from lorries parked on the commons, trenches were being dug across our parks and commons and there were notices telling us to keep out. Huge holes were being excavated in the parks and concrete poured in and we wondered why. Then notices went up announcing 'AIR RAID SHELTER', and this was sufficient to entice many children to explore the dark interiors of these man-made caverns.

I remember going to a hall or somewhere to be fitted with a gas-mask that the government said everyone should have. I went along with my parents, sister Betty and brother Jack and found that there were a lot of people waiting in the hall for their gas-masks. There were tables and some men were fitting the gas-masks on people and there was a smell of rubber in the air. Soon it was time for us to move to a table and my parents received theirs and then there was a 'Mickey Mouse' type for Jack and they wanted to give me one like that as well. I did not want one that was obviously a baby type, so I was fitted out with a similar one to my parents and Betty, who is older than me.

I do not remember anything about the train journey, or in deed whether we were told on the train what our destination was going to be. I do know that the train stopped at Bideford and that we all got off the train and went somewhere for food and drinks and that we were then put on buses and taken to Clovelly. The buses stopped at Clovelly Court, the manor house of the village and that somehow, Betty and I were taken to 'Temple Bar ', the cottage of Mr and Mrs George Lamey down the cobbled part of the village. Betty remembers an aunt (who had been an escort) not being there when we awoke on that first morning. She had left without saying goodbye and Betty was very upset about it, but I don't remember it at all.

This part of my stay in Clovelly and living with the Lameys is something that I do not remember much about, except that they were nice people, he was a fisherman and they had a grown up daughter. During my stay at 'Temple Bar', I had the most awful nightmares, something I had never suffered with before or since. Looking back on it now, it is perhaps natural that at that time I might be subject to nightmares; here I was a five year old, taken away from home and loving parents, albeit with an older sister to look after me, although she was only ten years old herself; and taken into a strange home in a part of the country I had never seen before and here were people speaking in an accent which must have appeared odd to me.

There came the time when schooling had to begin and because of some sort of trouble at the village school (Wrinkleberry) we could not go straight away and when we did, it was that Betty should go to the school whilst I and several other five/six year olds were to go to St. Peter's C of E chapel down in the village, which was turned into an emergency schoolroom.

After a while, Betty and I were moved, I don't know why, to live with Miss Jennings, who we always addressed as 'Miss' and who lived at Burscott in Higher Clovelly. This was among the farming community as opposed to the fisher folk down in Clovelly village. Miss Jennings was a maiden lady and her home was a small cottage in a group of five or six other cottages and two farms just off the main road to Clovelly village.

Now we no longer lived down in the village, I changed schools to the proper village school and was placed in Miss Cruse's class. Here at Wrinkleberry, we children were crammed in like sardines, with the younger children being in the two separate classes whilst there were three or four classes in the hall, with only curtains hung between each class. I was fortunate because as I got older, I moved from Miss Cruse's class to that of Miss Pam Williams, an evacuee teacher from Plymouth.

By this time in school, in addition to the thirtyfive to forty local children (five to fourteen years) there were about one hundred and fifty Londoner from Peckham and

Deptford, fifty from Bristol and fifty from Plymouth. In addition to the two local teachers, there were three from London, one from Bristol and one from Plymouth. The head teacher was Mr Hesketh who was the head before we came.

Teaching was necessarily loud at times, with the teachers raising their voices, not so much through anger, but to make themselves heard above the noise of the others. With only curtains between them, the other classes in the hall were always in difficulty where they might be reciting their multiplication tables as other were taking dictation or having reading lessons, and of course, the louder the noise was in the hall, the more we in the side classrooms could hear what they were doing. It was a bit inhibiting for us youngsters doing our two and three times tables, to hear the older ones reciting their twelve times table.

Even though we were in the depth of the country and supposedly cocooned from the war, we had our regular gas-mask drill in class, sometimes, doing a whole lesson

Dancing Class in 1941/42. From l to r, back row: (1) Gloria Pillman, (4) Jeanie Goulding
Middle row: (2) Alison Cavendish. On right (kneeling) Pat Reid
Front row: (3) Jill Gadd (4) Margaret Tridgell

whilst wearing the thing. It was not something that we liked, the nasty smell of rubber and the misting up of the eye-piece, made them at times to be something like an instrument of torture.

Another feature that remains with me is the stoves in each of the two rooms and the hall. These were huge iron stoves which burnt coke and were fenced in with high metal fireguards fixed to the wall, and each one had a bowl of water on top, which I understand was to remove the harmful fumes emanating from the fire; it also provided hot water for the teachers to wash their hands with at the end of classes.

Mouth Mill Cottage. 1940 At table: Eileen Law, Betty Gadd
Lying Down: Doreen Law, Gill Gadd

One thing that stands out in my mind was the visit to the school of the dentist. He came with a nurse and they occupied one of the side classrooms for the afternoon. Of course there was no proper dentist's chair, just an ordinary school chair, strong enough to stand the struggle of child, nurse and dentist. I do not recall having had any teeth extracted but I know that other children did, without any form of local anaesthetic. No one thought it a scandal, a war was on and everyone had to contribute something, even if it was only pain. Another thing to consider was that this all occurred in the early 1940's and would have been thought of as normal.

The playgrounds were separated for boys and girls and there was a four foot high stone wall surrounding the whole of the school area, with fields beyond which ran down to the woods, called the Hobby Woods and then down to the cliffs. It was a marvellous place to play in, except that as we seemed to play a lot of ball games, we were for ever climbing over the wall into the fields to retrieve our ball. As the boys appeared to spend more time in the fields than in the playground, we often called upon them to get our ball, but of course they would see that as an excuse to have a kick about and to tease us, letting us shout and shout until, fearing the intervention of Mr Hesketh, they would toss the ball back with ill grace.

There is a public footpath through the fields from Burscott to Wrinkleberry and this was a good short cut to school for all the children who lived near us. When the weather was wet we usually took the longer way by the road, otherwise our shoes would have got muddier than normal, not to

Betty and Jill Gadd on the bridge at Mouth Mill, Clovelly.
1941

Betty and Gill Gadd on the beach at Mouth Mill, Clovelly. 1940

mention wet feet. At each end of the footpath and at the hedges in between, there were wooden stiles that we had to climb over and this was another adventure because they were quite high for small children. If we set out or met up with another group of children, there would normally be races across the field to the next stile; at least that got us to school on time, a somewhat different proposition to when the blackberries were ripe on the hedges and were often too tempting to pass by, even if the school bell was ringing.

To help out the food with our foster parents rations, the education authorities had leased the old coach-house of the Rectory and converted it into a kitchen and canteen to supply lunch for the evacuees. It was not near to the school, being about one mile each way, and many children passed their foster homes in order to reach the canteen for their mid-day meal. We used to walk down Wrinkleberry Lane to the top of the village and then along the road to the canteen. Afterwards we would walk back on the main road, up Slerra Hill

to Wrinkleberry. I don't recall much about the place or the food, except that we queued, were served by ladies through a serving hatch and then took our meal through to another room to eat it at long tables.

Of course being in the country was new to most of us from London and many of us used our free time to

Betty and Gill Gadd on the beach at Mouth Mill, Clovelly. 1940

learn about nature and the names of trees and flowers. We were seeing for the first time and close-up, many animals we had only seen in our books. We got to stroke them and in many instances, to feed them and to know their ways. Another thing, the abundance of fresh vegetables and fruit is something that I will always remember, as most people had a garden attached to their cottage and as country people, they always grew a lot of their own vegetables and fruit; in any case, I understand that during the war, growing nothing but flowers in the garden was frowned upon and in most areas they had to be planted with food to help the war effort.

During this time in Clovelly I recall, there were two ladies who helped the children quite a lot, they were Miss Scott and her friend Miss Woodall. I believe they were friends of Mrs Asquith, who owned Clovelly then, because she let them use one of the large rooms above the stables, next to the squash court, to enable them to teach the girls dancing on Saturday mornings. I remember that we flocked to their lessons, mainly evacuees but there were some locals as well. These two ladies lived together in a little cottage at Burscott and nearby was a gentleman and his wife called Mr and Mrs Watson. He was a radio personality and used the name of Nosmo King, which he told us children that he had taken from the No Smoking sign in a railway carriage.

Miss Scott taught us the steps and how we should act and Miss Woodall played the gramophone from the small stage. We skipped and did exercises to music as well as dance routines and after a while they decided that we ought to appear in public to entertain the villagers. Some girls did put on a show, or were included in a show, but I don't think I took part, whether because I was too young or that I just did not want to. They were very nice ladies and I also remember that in addition to the dancing classes, they used to take Betty and I to church on Sundays and sometimes we would go with them to a cottage they rented at Mouth Mill. They often carried a camera with them and took quite a lot of photographs of children during their stay and for many, they were the only ones that were taken during those war years.

We loved going there because the cottage was about one hundred yards from the sea, was built on the side of a small stream, which had lots of trout swimming about in it and there was a good wooden bridge across the stream that we used to play on. They had nice lawns and gardens which went right up to the woods and the cliff tops, wild deer would come down from the woods and sometimes eat on the lawn and although we often waited and tried our hardest to see them, we never once caught a glimpse of them. Mouth Mill is noted locally for its rough seas in certain wind conditions and then the noise, even in the cottage is extremely loud. Other times we could play on a small stretch of sand between the large pebbles and dream about the stories the locals told, that smugglers always used Mouth Mill to bring their contraband ashore, where it would be loaded onto donkeys and spirited away over the hill-tops and through the woods to the hiding places before the Revenue men came.

When the wind was in a certain direction, pieces of wrecked ships or cargo would sometimes be washed up on the beach at Mouth Mill and with ships being sunk by German submarines and aircraft, there was always the chance of finding exciting things on the beach. Some people had found cases of oranges and these were well accepted gifts as they were more or less unknown by many children. I had never tasted grapefruit before that morning, when walking with Betty along the stoney beach, we spotted these things which I was told were grapefruits. Having tasted them I decided right away that I didn't like them, so it mattered not to me that there were none in the shops.

Living in a village that had the sea, boats and fishermen as well as the farms and countryside was special to the evacuees, sometimes when the weather was fine we would go down to the harbour for a swim or paddle in the water. The beaches at Clovelly are mainly pebbles and this presents problems for anyone walking in bare feet down to the water. We girls used to get changed in all sorts of places, some chose the boats that were up on the beach, others chose the old lime kiln with its dark seclusion whilst some of us opted to undress behind the wall by the cottages. Then we would stagger across the pebbles to the water and depending on how competent or confident we were, then walk in by the harbour and generally play about by the floating fishing boats.

I remember picking blackberries on one occasion with Betty and Eileen Law and I think it was in the Deer Park. This is not a public park but many acres of pasture and trees that belonged to Mrs Asquith and stretched from a green gate near the top of the cobbles, right along the cliff tops and then across to Clovelly Court. Mrs Asquith allowed her tenants to pick blackberries and nuts and other things in the Park as long as no damage was done and gates were shut, as she did over most of her property. On the day in question we were picking the blackberries and minding our own business when a group of boys came rushing up. They were panting and they gasped out the fact that they were being chased by some goats, screaming and pointing behind them. The shock and fright made us drop and spill our berries in the long grass and before the laughing boys could make off, Eileen had dealt with them. They would think twice before using that trick on us in the future.

Of course in rural areas like Clovelly in the early 1940's, there were no water mains, the household supply being taken from a pump or tap at the side of the road. Each pump or tap would have to serve as many as twenty homes and to see people carrying buckets of water along the road was a regular and common sight. Toilets were another thing that shocked most of the evacuees, they were not the flush type and were usually down at the bottom of the garden. Electricity was in the area but not many homes had it installed, depending instead on the paraffin lamps for their lighting, just as their parents had done before them.

Our parents came down to Clovelly to visit us in 1941 and they stayed at Dyke Green in Higher Clovelly, just up the road from us. They liked what they saw, inasmuch as we were happy, well cared for and healthy.

For some reason Betty and I left Burscott and went to live with Miss Jenning's brother and sister-in-law on a small farm in Slerra, Higher Clovelly. I don't remember much about my stay there except that Mr and Mrs Jennings had a daughter, Olive, who lived with them and that she was very nice to us. I can recall the first time I was placed on top of a large farm horse and being terrified because of the height I was from the ground. It was whilst we were staying at Slerra Farm, that I caught mumps. I suppose Mrs Jennings and Olive nursed me although I can't remember much about it.

About this time Betty left Clovelly School for the school in Bideford, Mrs Jennings became very ill and I was moved to live with the Rev. Cavendish and his wife at the Rectory. The Cavendish's lived in the huge old Rectory and their children were away at boarding school most of the time. It was a building with four levels of rooms, the large basements rooms which included the kitchen, the ground floor reception rooms, the family bedrooms on the first floor, and then on the upper floor, the staff rooms. It was here that I had my room, which I shared with another evacuee, named Ruth, who I believe came from Plymouth.

We did not see much of the Cavendish's except on Sunday. Ruth and I had our meals in the kitchen with cook and I remember that the room was very large and that there was a coffee grinder which was used for breakfast and evenings for the Cavendish's. I had never seen a coffee grinder before and I can still recall the lovely smell of coffee in that kitchen. There was another thing that fascinated me and that was the 'dumb waiter' lift that carried the food from the kitchen up to the dining-room above. There were lots of trees in the grounds and I was told that in a huge oak tree, the author, poet and cleric Charles Kingsley had played as a child, whilst living in the Rectory with his parents, his father being the Rector of Clovelly at the time, (1832 – 1836). This oak came to be know as the Kingsley oak and I believe it is still known as such.

It was here at the Rectory that I had my introduction to the game 'charades', which was played when the Cavendish children came home from boarding school at the Christmas break. Sometimes Mrs Cavendish would take me to Clovelly Court when she was going to visit Mrs Asquith as I believe they were friends. Walking across the grounds towards the manor house, I would often see people playing on the tennis courts and thought it grand to have your own tennis court. The Court gardens were large and surrounded by a high wall and inside were rows of glasshouses, many fruit trees and bushes and seemingly an abundance of vegetables and salad crops. Although there a large walled garden with the Rectory for vegetables and fruit, it appeared that Mrs Cavendish often got some of her supplies from the Court gardens.

It was in the driveway to Clovelly Court that I saw my first mass display of growing daffodils; they covered the ground on both sides of the road, and also on the bank opposite to the lodge. Being a girl from the big city, I thought they were wild and too good an opportunity to miss, so I picked an armful of them.

There came the time when the Cavendish's went away on holiday, possibly the summer of 1943, and I was taken across to Mr and Mrs Jim Cruse, the butcher, at the 'Retreat', which was on the Hartland road and about one and a half miles from the school. I enjoyed myself with them, he was a large man with a red cheery face and she was kind. They already had two other London evacuees, Jeannie Goulding and Pat Reid and we were all about the same age. We got on well together and before it was time for me to return to the Cavendish's, I ask Mr Cruse if I could stay with them all at the 'Retreat' and not go back to the Rectory. The answer was swift and readily given, Yes I could stay with them. Butcher Cruse and his wife became Uncle Jim and Auntie Rose to me and they gave me a wonderful home.

The Cruse's had three daughters, Barbara, who was the infants' teacher at Wrinkleberry, Mary, who was in the A.T.S., and Joan who worked with her father in the butchery business. Upstairs, two of us children slept in the small room, whilst the other slept with Joan in a big bed, in fact we took it in turns to sleep with Joan. We must have liked sleeping with her, I suppose it was because she was an adult and she was so friendly, although, I wonder now what she thought of having strange evacuees sleeping with her each night. Maybe I'll ask one day.

I remember once, the Cruse's took us to the next village, Bucks Cross, to a social and this was something new to me, although socials were very much part of the village life in those days. A cross between a proper dance and a games night for children, they attracted people of all ages and allowed parents to take their children along to join in. There would be a three or four piece band and everyone took part in a variety of things from games, to old fashioned dances. It was always considered to be a fun night.

On this occasion we travelled over in Uncle Jim's little van and it must have been a special treat because we were allowed to stay up until nine o'clock and as there were usually sandwiches, cold pies and lemonade, we had a very good time and everyone seemed so happy.

One thing that happened at this social was that in a sketch, a group of local men were on a wooden plank placed across a trestle see-sawing up and down. Whilst they were doing this they were singing 'Widdecombe Fair' and I suppose at some point they put a little more effort into their up and down motions which suddenly caused the plank to snap and scattered the men across the floor. We children roared with laughter but on reflection, I don't think it was meant to be and someone could have been hurt.

After this, we often (perhaps monthly) went to other socials which were held in the school, there being no village hall at the time, or in Long Passage at Clovelly Court. The ones at the Court were usually in aid of the Red Cross or Parcels for the Troops, in fact whether it was at the Court or school, they were all in aid of something, so that everyone contributed to the war effort.

Uncle Jim was a Methodist lay preacher and Auntie Rose sometimes played the organ at the nearby chapel called Providence, which is on the Hartland road. We would go with them and at the chapel, we children went up the stone steps on the outside, to a room above the chapel, where there was a Sunday school. Sometimes because Uncle Jim was preaching in a different village, we would go with him and meet the people in that chapel and attend a different Sunday school.

Now we were at 'Retreat', it was much further to walk to school and usually in addition to Jeannie, Pat and myself, there would be children from the nearby farms and cottages coming along at the same time until there could be quite a bunch of us, then Auntie Barbara would pass us on her bicycle and tell us not to dawdle and be late for school. Sometimes on the way home, especially if we were not too many, the Post Office van on its way to Hartland, would stop and give us a lift to the gate of 'Retreat'.

There came the time when I was aware that Auntie Barbara had a rented cottage down by the 'Look Out' in Clovelly village. I remember that you could look out of the windows and see right across the bay and if the sea was rough, see the white line of foam where the waves broke over Bucks Gore, which are a line of rocks extending out from the beach at Buck Mills, just along the coast from Clovelly. We girls used to go down to visit Auntie Barbara there and sometimes have tea with her. Of course going down the cobbles, past all the pretty in cottages, brought back all the memories I had of my early days in Clovelly.

One little story that I remember, is being asked by Auntie to ask a lady and a gentleman, who were sitting on a seat on the quay, for their autographs. I said that I couldn't.(I was too shy). I don't know if one of the other girls asked for their autographs, as autograph books were all the rage with lots of children at that time. I discovered later that the lady and gentleman were Anne Zeigler and Webster Booth, the singers.

I remember when the Wellington bomber crashed near to West Dyke Farm in Higher Clovelly. It happened one night and I believe it exploded when it hit the ground and all the crew were killed. It crashed through two hedges, on each side of the lane along which we walked to school, and the wreckage was in the two fields on each side. I know that a day or so later, when we walked past on our way home from school, there were a lot of airman and soldiers sorting through the pieces of the 'plane and loading them on lorries. I remember they were friendly and one of them calling out, "Hello blondie "in what I thought was an American accent, but of course it could have been Canadian. I had never heard the phrase 'Blondie' called out before and was not sure whether or not I liked it.

Uncle Jim rented a few fields at the bottom of Slerra hill from the Clovelly Estate and I remember being in some of these when the crop was being harvested. As a special treat we were allowed to climb in the van and hold steady the baskets of food and drinks that would be given to the men who were harvesting; then they let us sit down by the hedge with them and share the food. We thought it was great fun to have our tea in the fields with the men.

October 1943 has a special place in my memory, for on the 21 October, Auntie Joan married a soldier named John Searles and we three London evacuee girls were to be the bridesmaids. Joan had met Johnny locally, for he was stationed on a searchlight or gun site near to Clovelly Cross in Higher Clovelly. We girls were taken to a dressmaker in Hartland to have our dresses made for us, pretty pale blue material with white net over and with puffed sleeves. To crown it we wore juliet caps, new black shiny shoes and white socks. We were especially good at this time, our behaviour being monitored and we having been told that if we were not good, others could be found to take our place.

During the winters I spent as an evacuee in Clovelly, I experienced snow like I had never done before. Whether they were particularly bad winters I don't know, but they were definitely different from anything we had had in London. No doubt this could be attributed to the open spaces which attract high winds but the snow was very deep all over the roads and fields. For us children it gave us so much scope for play, until our hands and feet got too cold to remain outside any longer. I remember we used to make enormous snowballs in the fields, just rolling them and rolling them until they got as big as we were. I have a photograph somewhere of Betty and myself where we are standing in a lane that had just been cleared of snow. If my memory is correct, pixie hood hats, wellington boots and thick coats were de rigueur for Clovelly winters in the early 40's.

The 'Retreat', where we lived, was also where Uncle Jim carried on his business as a butcher and often when the big delivery lorry had completed the unloading of his meat, the driver had had his cup of tea and he would be preparing to travel on to Hartland with his next delivery, he would turn to us girls and invite us to have a ride into Hartland and back. We needed no second invitation and would clamber up into the back, along with all the meat carcasses and the lorry would go on its way with us swinging and bumping about with the meat. I think the driver liked to hear us screaming and squealing with delight at the adventure. After making his delivery in Hartland, the driver would drop us off outside the gate of 'Retreat' before continuing on his way home. Somehow, I don't think it would be permitted nowadays.

Letters from my parents were something that were eagerly awaited every week, and of course like all the other evacuees, letter writing was something that we had to learn at an early stage. I shudder to think what my letters were like and I know that I was not alone in my lack of proficiency at letter writing. One lady that I know, admitted that when she was a little girl, her letter to her parents ended with "… and God blast you". My mother sent me parcels as often as she could and I looked forward to them as they usually contained new clothes and goodies and comics and I remember that Auntie Rose was for ever amazed that the shoes that my mother sent, always fitted.

In 1944, my mother came down with my brother to live in Bideford, and they stayed for quite a long time, I suppose it was because of the V1 and V2 raids, but at least the feeling was that it was getting near the end of the war.

Because it was such a small village, Clovelly had never had any childrens' or youth organisations such as the Scouts or Guides, even when the place was bursting at the seams with children during the early part of the war. So it was quite unexpected when it was announced that they were going to form a Brownie pack in Clovelly. Many girls joined, but as I was expected to be returning to London in the very near future, I was not allowed to join. I was bitterly disappointed in not being allowed to be a Brownie and this was not helped, when next day at school, the lucky girls punished me with stories of how marvellous the first meeting had been and what a lovely time they had all had. I suppose at that very moment, I hated everyone and didn't really want to join the rotten Brownies. Later however, I was determined to join when I got back to London, but fate intervened, for when I got there and after the usual enquiries had been made, I discovered that there were no plans for setting up a Brownie pack locally. Later, when things got back to some normality I joined the Girl Guides and as I expected, enjoyed myself immensely.

Then came the time for my return home to Peckham. There were lots of tears when saying good bye to my friends and of course, Auntie Rose and Uncle Jim, Auntie Joan and Auntie Barbara. My mother had returned to London, as well as my sister Betty and now it was my turn. My leaving was a mixture of sadness and happiness, with the excitement of going home to my family again. I was given a little Spaniel puppy as a memento of my stay in Clovelly and I called her Vicky. My parents knew nothing about Vicky until I arrived with her and they made a fuss of her. Sadly, Vicky caught distemper shortly afterwards and died, maybe as she was a country dog she could not settle in London.

When I arrived at Waterloo railway station on that day in 1945, I was met by my parents, Betty and my brother, then home to Maxted Road. There across the front of the house was a banner, on which was written, 'Welcome home Betty and Jill', although Betty had arrived home earlier than me. Then it was a time of settling in, re-learning the old streets and seeing the familiar names once more. I was told I would be returning to Bellenden Road school once again, but this time in the Juniors.

I recall going back to the school for my first day. The school looked huge and dirty, the fire escape stairs that zig-zagged up the side of the building was to be our main entrance for the Juniors, which was on the top (third) floor of the school. Oh dear, it was so different from little Wrinkleberry, but I would have to get used to it as well as a new collection of school friends.

There were other things to see and explore in the area near to my house; the bomb sites and either gaps in terraces that I had known or whole streets that had disappeared, leaving only dreary spaces of soil and rubble. Thankfully a lot of these sites were soon tidied up and strange little houses built on them, like overgrown chicken houses, in rows with small gardens and a wire fence around. As the houses had been made in factories and then assembled on the sites, they were called 'Pre Fabs' and they soon became welcome additions to the neighbourhood with pretty little gardens. I used to think that they seemed nicer than our little terrace houses, and I believe that although originally they were only intended to last for a small number of years, in many instances they were still being lived in some thirty years later.

CHAPTER SIX

EARWIGS AND CARBUNCLES

In the years that this story covers, nobody would have believed that about fifty years later, the events concerning me, Raymond Lamb , would be recorded in writing. This is my story.

When the war started in 1939 I was eight years of age and lived with my mother and father at 39, Elm Grove, Peckham in south London. My school was Bellenden Road Elementary School, which was a large building on two floors and held a few hundred children. It was mixed boys and girls in the Junior part and also a separate gate and playground for the Infants.

When it was announced over the radio and in the school that there was to be an evacuation, my mother and father discussed it quite a bit. I remember that for several evenings it would be mentioned off and on. They were trying to weigh up the possible danger from German bombs with the perils of allowing me to go off to someone, we knew not where, and with the minimum of supervision from some teachers – who, had not yet been decided.

Mum would say, "I agree with you Bert, we just don't know what sort of people will take him in. For all we know they mightn't feed him properly or keep him clean and you know what boys are like, but we can't keep him here if Hitler's lot start bombing us."

Dad's view was that if I stayed at home, we would all be together, I would be looked after and they knew where I was. He normally gave in to mum's wishes anyway and would say, "All right Rose, if that's what you really want for the boy, but we've got to tell them at the school that we want to know as much about where he's going to stay as they know. I don't want him just being sent off to the country and we don't know where he is." I really do not know what answer my mother got from the school authorities but I do know that she was influenced by the happening around the world at that time.

We had all seen the Pathe and GB. News films in the cinema, of the bombing in China, Spain and Poland. We knew that the Germans were already bombing different parts of England, like the ports and airfields and wondered when they would reach London. The horror of the mass bombing was in our minds, because of the films and no doubt that played a big part in persuading my parents, particularly my mother, in registering my name to be evacuated.

War-time London, before we went away, had altered dramatically from the London that I had grown to know. Peckham was one of the southern boroughs of London and it bordered, in those days on areas of open air and greenery. At the other end of Peckham, there was the canal which ran from the River Thames and was about a mile from the docks at Deptford. My home in Elm Park was nearer to the docks than the open spaces to the south and if there was to be much bombing of the docks, then it was the part of Peckham that would get hit. All across, in zig-zag lines, trenches had been dug on Peckham Rye Common. Air-raid shelters dug through the turf, others built in the streets and sandbags being put up in great walls outside lots of public buildings. Hugh rectangular metal reservoirs had been placed in certain streets and then filled with water as emergency water supply depots. A familiar sight was London taxis towing two-wheeled water pumps around and crewed by men in steel helmets and boiler suits. These had been commandeered by the government and were part of the A.F.S. (Auxiliary Fire Service) to supplement the London Fire Brigade.

For children that were adventurous enough to go out and experience these new 'playthings' that the authorities had thoughtfully dotted about the area, was something not to be missed. Gangs of boys would decend on the trenches, which although seven to eight feet deep, gave realistic additions to the imagination of the young. Many fierce battles were fought and won in the muddy reaches of the trenches on Peckham Rye.

The air-raid shelters provided somewhere to explore, even though most of them were water-logged and as time progressed, smelly. In the end the shelters were not places to play in, they were reserved as our 'prisons' for children the gang did not like or had fallen out with. It did not take long for the authorities to come to the same conclusion as many of us, that people were using the shelters for purposes other than what they were intended for. Consequently wooden gates were placed across the entrances of all underground and surface shelters, fastened with padlock and chain, the keys being kept by one of the street or area air-raid wardens.

The black-out was another war time experience that many people would have been glad to miss. Motor vehicle crawling along with just the faintest of lights shining. White circles painted on lamp posts and trees that bordered the kerb edge. Kerbs and entrances to many public buildings also had white paint markings, all in an attempt to prevent people injuring themselves in the black-out. Curtains or shutters on the windows of the house were another thing, with the police or the air-raid wardens shouting out or knocking on the door if they saw a glimmer of light coming from the house.

It was on the 14 June 1940, that all the children that went to my school and were going to be evacuated, had to-attend Bellenden Road School with their belongings. It was a fine sunny morning when we set off along Bellenden Road from school, each child with a label tied with string to a coat, blouse or jumper and carrying his bag, case or brown paper parcel. Marching in columns like the army with teachers and escorts shepherding us along. We turned right into Blenheim Grove, which was the next street to mine, and up to the end of Blenheim Grove to the railway station. Following us along on the pavement were the mums and some onlookers. There were shouts of

"Goodbye love "; "Look after Billy ";" Be a good girl" and a hundred other calls. Handkerchiefs were out, people were crying and then we were moved swiftly into the station and up onto the platform, where a train was waiting for us.

Like many other things that happened that day, I cannot remember the train journey. I know it was long, hot and tiring and that we stopped once to have food and drinks that was laid out on the platform for us and that there were lots of ladies serving us. We eventually arrived at Bideford and after more food and a wash, we were put on buses and brought to Clovelly. There were two schools in our party of about one hundred and fifty children, there was ours from Peckham and the other one was from Deptford.

At Clovelly Court, the manor house, we all got out and stood in lines. I thought that Clovelly Court was a beautiful house and throughout my stay in Clovelly I remained in awe of the place. There were lots of people waiting for us and they starting walking along the rows of children, reading what was on the labels then looking at the child. If there was a brother and a sister or two brothers or sisters, they stood holding hands to indicate they were together. Most of the children who had a younger one to look after were under the strictest of orders from their parents that they were not to be separated under any circumstances. This of course caused many problems when some of the ladies that were coming forward to accept us, were not prepared to take in a small child with all its attendant problems.

Eventually I found myself standing in the cool semi-darkness of a cottage with an elderly lady welcoming me. I remember I was thirsty and I asked for a glass of water and was amazed to see it poured out of a stone pitcher instead of the tap. Where was the tap, I wondered. I was soon to discover that this was the country and in rural areas such as Clovelly in the early 1940's, there were no such things as water taps in the home.

Other things that I had been used to and had taken for granted, was a flush water toilet in the house and electricity. I discovered to my horror that no such ordinary necessities of life existed in many of the homes in Clovelly at this time, the toilet for our cottage was in a little shed situated about thirty yards down the road and that it was not a flush one. No toilet paper, just squares of newspaper tied up with string and hung on a nail on the inside of the door. This really was primitive living and I, as well as the other children, were just not prepared for it. No one had prepared us as to what we should find and have to get used to, so I suppose it took the teachers by surprise as well. My view then was, "O God I shall never survive this."

Although I grew to love the place, I never did get used to not having any electricity in the house, that easily switched on light. My new home had oil lamps for lighting downstairs, with candles to carry to see yourself around upstairs. Each had its problems and techniques. I soon found that if the weather was windy, unless you shielded the flame of the candle, it would go out. It matter not that you were in doors because nothing fitted properly and old coats were called into service to act as draught stoppers. Other surprises were to follow on top of each other.

I think most people's idea of the countryside were green fields with animals eating grass. Sometimes the fields might be brown, othertimes they might be golden with corn. We knew that milk came from a cow and that hens laid eggs. Being close up to a cow was a new thing for most of us but not the same with horses, as we had hundreds of them in London and would see them every day.

The lady that had taken me in was Mrs Charlotte Bartlett, who was a lady in her sixties and she lived with her daughter Lottie, who was about thirtyfive and single, although she had a boy friend and hoped soon to get married. Their home was a little thatched cottage on the main road from Clovelly Cross to Clovelly village, and it was also opposite to the little lane that led to the village school which was about a quarter of a mile away.

At first there was no room for us at the school and we used to walk around the lanes and woods with our teachers, learning all about the flowers and trees and all aspects of nature. Fortunately the weather was mostly fine and on the odd occasions that it rained, we went into a farmer's barn and stood around whilst the teacher taught us a subject. It was from these many nature walks that I got my love of the countryside and my knowledge of nature. Even when we started at school, there were no pencils or paper for us and some of us were provided with slates to write on.

The Hon.Mrs Betty Asquith and her daughters lived at Clovelly Court and they made the evacuees so very welcome and throughout the war, Mrs Asquith gave the children a fairly free run of the grounds and made one or two rooms available in the house, in which she organised parties and games for us. I can still remember the wonderful times she and her staff gave us, even on war-time rations she still managed to find sufficient to give us children a wonderful time. She was a widow and all of her daughters were adults, although one might have been a teenager, and in addition to giving us so much, she also took in several boys from the Deptford school. Her husband had been Brigadier Asquith, the son of Herbert Asquith, the one time Prime Minister. Mrs Asquith was the daughter of Lord and Lady Manners of Avon Tyrell. In 1941, Clovelly Court was turned into a Red Cross Convalescent Home and sadly whilst it was in that use, much of it was accidentally destroyed by a fire that swept through part of the house. That was the end to any more parties, dances or whist drives being held in the Long Passage.

The school at Clovelly was at the end of a little lane opposite to Mrs Bartlett's cottage and was sited among a few cottages and a farm in a beautiful place named Wrinkleberry. Everyone called it Wrinkleberry School and it was a place where the old system of learning was carried on, including the punishment. Mr Hesketh, the Head Teacher, was helped by teachers from London, Bristol and Plymouth, as well as Miss Barbara Cruse from Clovelly. It was pretty well packed out when we Londoners joined in with the local children, but when the Bristol evacuees and then a group from Plymouth came as well, it was jam packed with no proper partitions between classes in the hall, except curtains.

For the older boys there was a welcome relief to get out of the school and dig for victory. The school had a garden along the lane and then took over a grassy plot to cultivate. We grew lots of vegetables and fruit for the school canteen in the old rectory coach-house. In addition to digging at school, I had taken over the two gardens of Mrs

Bartlett, to save her the hard work of gardening. This I continued to do right up until I left.

One night whilst I was asleep in bed I was woken up by a sound of banging and it seemed that I was being hit on the head with a hammer. It was so frightening that I ran downstairs calling out for help. Was I going mad I thought. I could not make out what it was. Mrs Bartlett tried to calm me but the noise was excruciating and I did not know what was causing it. Eventually Mrs Bartlett discovered that an ear-wig was inside my ear and it did not take her long, with me lying sideways on the kitchen table, to get the ear-wig out with her hairpin. She reckoned it must have dropped down from the thatch through the open window onto my pillow. Although I was always wary of ear-wigs in my room after that, I never saw any more and my experience of that one was sufficient. I now listen sceptically when naturalists state that stories of ear-wigs liking for human ears is a fallacy.

If the ear-wig incident did not necessitate medical attention, my carbuncle did. This was some weeks after my introduction to night prowling ear-wigs and no hairpin of Mrs Bartlett was going to take it away. The carbuncle was on my neck and it appeared to be huge. So off I was sent to see the District Nurse who lived in a little cottage next to the Post Office at Turn Pike in Higher Clovelly. Nurse Pinch soon took me in hand and had me sitting in a chair in her cottage whilst she busied herself getting the instruments ready, behind my back. She was not very big but she was powerful and with one hand she held my neck like it was in a vice, and with the other hand she lanced the carbuncle. It was a good thing that I could not see what she was about to do, I might have bolted had I seen her blade. Within a few minutes she had dealt with the problem, dressed it and sent me on my way home again.

I was soon introduced into the parish church and for Sunday School as well. After a while I agreed to pump the organ in church, but I found that this was a hasty decision on my part. Having agreed to do the job, I soon found it a bit of a drag having to attend church in all weathers for Matins and Evening Prayer to pump the organ, as well as go to Sunday school in the afternoon.

My job was to see that there was the required amount of wind pressure for the organ to operate at all times and I would pump away at the huge set of bellows that were fixed on the side of the organ for this purpose. It necessitated me sitting in a squashed position between the organ and the wall, out of sight of the congregation but in view of the rector, Rev. Cavendish and the organist, Mr Tom Finch, in deed within reach of the organist. Once during a particularly long and boring service I fell asleep over the handle of the bellows. When the Mr Finch started to play the next hymn, there was insufficient wind to operate it, so he rudely awakened me with a very vicious kick. Two things that I would like to mention about my spell as the organ-pumper in All Saints Church, Clovelly, is that I have always disliked organ music ever since and that for this task I was paid the princely sum of sixpence each week and threepence extra if there was a wedding or a funeral.

To help out with the food rations, a gang of us boys, local as well as evacuees, used to go out on the cliff and collect sea-gull eggs which were all right as long as you did not mind them being slightly fishy. The locals had taught me how to set snares to catch rabbits and one or two farmer allowed me to put the snares in their fields. In return I would trap the moles in their fields and these I would skin and send away, always hoping for them to be graded as Class 1, in which case I would get sixpence for each skin. By this time I was becoming a proper country boy and because I wanted to, I learnt fast.

We gangs of boys used to play soldiers both in the playground and in the fields and woods. In the playground our favourite game was usually a very violent one which we called Stalingrad. A group of boys, usually those in Harry Clement's gang, would form one or two lines across a corner of the playground, from wall to wall and defend it. The corner was Stalingrad. All the rest of the boys in the playground would then attack and attempt to break through the lines to capture Stalingrad. It was very rough and those who were faint hearted did not join in. I remember that those defending Stalingrad used the names of some of the Russian generals that we heard on the radio or read in the newspapers. It was a good game but we usually came out of it with a few bruises and it was our way of letting off steam. In our quieter moments and just talking among ourselves, we used to vow that the Germans would never take Clovelly without paying dearly, and of course, there was always the Home Guard.

The Home Guard was, I expect, just like those in other areas of Britain at that time. They had all sorts of occupations, mainly to do with farming or fishing. Some were ex-servicemen from the 1914-1918 War and looked the part with their rifle and uniform, but others who had never been in any group or organisation that wore uniform, looked comical, almost as if they were not part of it, even the locals had a chuckle over them. One such chap lived a few doors away from us, I think he was a bank clerk and nowadays every time I watch the television show of 'Dad's Army' I am reminded of him.

They used to patrol the cliff-tops, the beaches and the woods along our part of the coast. I know that they maintained an observation post at Mouth Mill and that place can be extremely cold in the winter, especially when the wind is from the north. When I think of them now, I marvel in the fact that they worked all day at their usual job, and both farming and fishing can be long hard hours, and then they would spend the best part of the night out on patrol. Thankfully the Germans did not decide to land on our part of the coast.

Because labour was short, we boys were asked to work on the land in our holidays and once we had reached twelve years of age, we could take time off from school for the purpose of helping in the corn and potato harvest. I always enjoyed working at corn harvest, the horse and carts that came into the fields empty, were loaded with high wobbly stacks of sheaves and then go on back to the farm yard for the corn to be built into ricks. I loved the meal breaks because we would all sit down by the hedge and eat the food that the women had brought out to the fields. Although very tired we would all be hungry and the lovely food was just what we had been waiting for, there was also cider for the men and lemonade for the boys.

In the winter, the steam threshing machine would come around to the various farms to thresh the corn from the ricks. That was a dirty and noisy job and normally only done by men and land army girls, the children would have to keep clear of the machinery. However they would let us near when the rick was nearly finished and only about a few feet of it left, then we would have the wire-netting around the rick, get the dogs and sticks and kill any rat that came out and there usually were plenty.

Mostly I helped out on the farm next door to the cottage, that was Mr and Mrs Jim Bragg and he taught me to milk cows, how to feed the stock, removing maggots from the hooves of sheep, then disinfecting the wounds.

This was the time that I fell in love. She was a bubbly girl from Peckham and I was head over heels in love with her but I don't think she knew it. She was such a kind girl and always seemed to be happy so I suppose that was what attracted her to me. I know her name and where she lives but I will refrain from mentioning her name in case it embarrasses her.

I remember the time that the Canadians soldiers came to stay in Clovelly. There were not many, maybe about twenty of them with an officer. We thought they had been sent by the government to reinforce our gang in Clovelly. Anyway the Canadian were specialists and were climbing the cliffs, even Gallantry Bower, which many locals had said was unclimbable. I remember being given a ride in a Bren-gun carrier one day, we went down the back road to the quay and then they brought me up again in a 15 cwt. truck. I thought that was the tops, it was terrific. They used to practice climbing the cliffs every day and also used rocket propelled grappling hooks and ropes to get up the cliffs swiftly and they would go where we boys would not dare to go. They only stayed a matter of weeks and were billeted with local families in the area. Soon after they left, there was the Allied raid on Dieppe, where many Canadian fought and died and I think that one local family heard afterwards that most of those we had made friends with in Clovelly had died in the landing. I often think of them, the kindness they showed the children and the chocolates they gave us.

Mrs Bartlett's daughter Lottie had a boy friend who was in the Home Guard and I remember once that he said that a German plane had crash landed nearby and that the Home Guard had to guard it until it could be taken away. I know that I asked him for a piece of the plane as a souvenir and he brought me back a piece of one of the propellers.

We used to watch the convoys of ships sailing along the coast past Clovelly, most times with barrage balloons above them. Once or twice I saw German planes attacking them and could see the puffs of smoke in the sky as the anti-aircraft guns on the ships fired back at the planes. I remember once when a German fighter plane fired on the harbour and village. I was not down there at the time, but next day the children who had been there were all telling stories about it and apparently a Royal Navy motor launch, that was anchored just off the quay, fired back at the German plane and it crashed into the sea near Mouth Mill. The lifeboat went out and brought the German pilot back, he was alive and I believe uninjured.

Living in a village like Clovelly gave you the best of both worlds, the countryside and the sea. When we were not playing or working in the fields we would go down to the harbour and swim and fish. I remember my first fishing experience, when I was fishing from the top of the quay, but not for long. Somehow or other I caught a fishing hook in my hand and the more I tried to get it out the more it became embedded in until it was right in deep. I was yelling and I suppose dancing about a bit until two of the local fishermen looked up from where they were working and saw that I needed help. Up the steps from their boat they came, wearing their waders, blue jersey and peaked caps. They examined the hand, clucked their tongues and shook their heads and then whilst one held me and the hand steady, the other pulled out the fish hook. Lesson one, they told me, was for the hook to go into the mouth of the fish and not the fisherman's hand. I vowed to leave fishing to the experts, and in Clovelly there were plenty of them. Nowadays, when people ask me about this incident I tell them that I threw the line behind me and over my shoulder to cast, and caught an idiot.

About this time, Aunt Lottie died. She had gone to the next village of Hartland to have her teeth seen to. I think the dentist pulled some teeth out and she came home. A few days later she became very ill and within a day or so she died. It was said that her death was attributed to the treatment she received at the dentist. Of course, in those days, nothing was done about it and everyone said what a terrible thing it was, and that was the end of it. I was very sad about this as Aunt Lottie had been good fun to be with, she played games with me and showed me a lot of affection. I think that being with Mrs Bartlett at this time gave her some comfort and the loss of her daughter was so sudden and traumatic.

View from school playground at Wrinkleberry

At times I must have been a nasty little boy because I can remember one incident where I hurt a girl, an evacuee from Deptford whose name was Georgina Hunt. It came about as we were walking along together and I was pontificating on my newly acquired knowledge of nature. I told her that the stinging nettles did not sting that month and to prove my point, I carefully picked some and she, trusting me, held out her bare arm and I rubbed the nettles up and down, with the obvious consequences. Not satisfied with that, as she cried in pain, I pushed her into the bed of nettles and ran away. I know that Georgina has never forgotten that incident and although she cannot remember who did this to her, she finds it hard to forgive the boy, and who can blame her for my actions were horrible. I confess to Georgina now, that I was the guilty one.

As if in retribution, I was grabbed one day in the woods by a gang of boys and tied upside down to a tree. It was not for what I had done to Georgina, but no doubt I had upset someone who was taking his revenge whilst he had enough with him to carry it out. I remember that there were other children nearby so when the gang left me tied to the tree, it was not long before someone came along and cut me down. Time has faded the memory of who the boys were, but after such a length of time, does it really matter.

The meals cooked by Mrs Bartlett were really good and even with war-time food restrictions, she always seemed to fill my plate at meal times. The food was so lovely, all local recipes, potato pasty, leek pasty or pie, beautiful stews which would contain rabbit or sometimes a bit of meat from the butcher. Potato, parsley and cream pie with junket and cream to follow. Mrs Bartlett did what all the ladies did with their junkets – she grated nutmeg over the top of the junket just before she served it. I remember her getting a big pan of milk and putting it on top of the oven for a little while, then taking it away into the pantry to cool off until the next day. Then she would skim off the beautiful thick clotted cream and layer it into a glass dish. That would be served with the junket, or with bread and jam, which was a local favourite. In the summer, the cream would be served with strawberries or other soft fruit and then in the autumn with blackberry and apple pie.

All this was cooked in an oven heated mainly by wood. there was a small coal ration, which did not go far, so it was necessary to get wood. Mrs Asquith allowed her villagers to pick fallen wood from the woods on her estate and most villagers could be seen staggering along with a branch on their shoulders. This was particularly so after a gale.

In addition to picking blackberries from the hedges, we also used to pick rose hips, and there were plenty of wild roses growing all around Clovelly. These were turned into rose-hip syrup by Mrs Bartlett and was useful for treating colds in the winter.

Early in 1944, my parents decided that as the raids had stopped, it would be safe for me to return home. This was a wrench for I had been with Mrs Bartlett for nearly four years, had grown fond of her and the way of life in Clovelly. Mrs Bartlett, in her turn, had shown me much love and affection and I would be sorry to part from her and my little bedroom in the thatched cottage. I loved my parents but I did not really want to go home to London. My mother and father told me that they missed me badly, that our home was still intact and that my bedroom was waiting for me, just like it was before I left in 1940. I know that I also missed my parents and for this reason I suppose, I agreed that I should return.

Peckham had changed a lot in the four years that I had been away. Shops, streets and places that I knew so well had gone with just a pile of bricks and rubble to mark their spot. Within a week of returning home, the air-raid sirens started up again as the 'doodlebug' V1 bombs started coming over. Of course this was an excuse for me to say to my parents, "What have you brought me back to?". The raids by the V1's and then the V2's caused a lot of damage to many parts of London and the counties to the south of London. Our own home was severely damaged but thank goodness no one was in the house when it was hit. Although we survived this bombing, I regretted many times that I had ever left Clovelly.

As the weeks went by, I slowly got used to being in London again, the noise and smells were different and for a boy there were some wonderful places to play. Piles of rubble that were once the homes of people now dead or moved away, but to a young boy they were adventure grounds. Thinking back on it now, I realised how dangerous it was, when, finding a slight opening to a cellar, we would drag bricks away until we had room to struggle through and then explore the darkness beneath the rubble. Many of the cellars still had household items in them and I think that made us stop and think about the war again.

Other times I would hunt and find shrapnel and these could always be swapped around with other boys, and if you had some writing on the piece of metal, you would be able to distinguish between German and British casings, bomb or anti-aircraft shell. I know that with the occasional building being destroyed by the bombs, I was suddenly concerned that the little sweet shop on the corner would survive to supply me with my two ounces of sweets each week.

I must add that my formative years in Clovelly, surrounded by much kindness, was good for me and has stood me in good stead ever since.

CHAPTER SEVEN

EARS AND NITS

I don't know what others have written about their being evacuated as children to Clovelly in North Devon in 1940. For some, in fact many, it was a good time and they had very happy billets and wanted to stay on, but for a few of us, our time in Clovelly was marred by unfriendly foster parents who gave us the barest minimum of care and attention.

In 1940 my name was Dene Grice and I lived with my mum and dad, Amy and Bill Grice at 135, Chadwick Road, Peckham in south London. My school was quite near, Bellenden Road Elementary School and most of my school friends lived in the streets close to me. I was a family loving girl, very quiet and one who doted on her parents, who showered me with love. I was different to what I am now; then I was very shy and could easily be bullied and put upon by others, although it seemed that it was only adults that made me suffer.

My dad was in the Royal Navy at around the time it came for our names to be put forward on the evacuation register and I know that my mum was reluctant for me to leave her. I was only ten years old and she knew, like all parents, that I would be safer in the countryside, away from London if the bombing was going to be anything like we had been seeing on the news reels in the cinema. There we had seen the bombing of China by the Japanese, the bombing of towns and cities in Spain and the bombing in Poland. If London was expected to get the same, then we were going to suffer. However, very reluctantly, my mum filled in the application form for me to take to school and to have my name added to the register.

My mum's fear, which she repeated over and over again, was that she did not know what sort of place I would be sent to. Who would there be to make certain that I was being looked after properly. Neither the school nor the education authorities could answer to her satisfaction, being merely told that there would be plenty of supervision by the Billeting Officers in the reception areas. She could not understand why no one could tell her where we would be going.

The date for our departure was announced and I well remember the night before with my mother crying and cuddling me. Then as she was getting me ready to go in the morning she had a good cry again. Off I went to the school with my suitcase and gas mask and my mum had added a bar of chocolate, a packet of crisps and a few pennies in my pocket.

We got on the train at Peckham Rye Railway Station but I don't remember saying good bye to my mother, there were crowds of people, children and parents shouting out to each other, whilst the teachers and escorts tried to get the children along to the platform without losing too many.

I don't remember very much about the train journey except that I know that it stopped at Exeter and there the WVS. ladies, wearing long white aprons, and with tables loaded with cakes, sandwiches and drinks for us. After a while, on we went again until we reached Bideford, although the name did not mean much to us at the time. Here we got off the train and there were lots of people to help us carry our cases and things. We had a wash and then some more food and drinks and were put onto buses.

We guessed this was the final part of our journey, maybe someone told us that we were going to Clovelly, but I don't remember. The buses stopped in front of a huge house, with big lawns and grounds sloping towards the sea, and a crowd of women and some men started to come forward. When we got out of the buses we were lined up in rows and I can recall the people coming forward and looking at us, reading what our name and age was from the label that was tied on our clothes. There were people, who were probably in charge, who had sheaves of papers in their hands, and occasionally a child or a pair of children would go off with someone. I remember a soft spoken lady coming up to me and being very kind and asked me if I wanted a drink of anything. One woman asked me if I had a little brother or a sister with me as she preferred to have related children. At the time I was an only child so I was coupled up with a little girl, three years younger than me by the name of Valerie Goatley.

The lady who had spoken to me and who eventually took Valerie and me away with her was called Mrs Howard. We had a long walk along the road under the trees until we got to the top of a very steep hill. It was all cobbles and there were a few people walking down in front of us, some with evacuee children, who no doubt, like me, wondered where on earth we had come to. We soon arrived at her home, half-way down the steep street at 98, High Street. Here Mrs Howard introduced us to her mother, who was very old, and who was sitting in a chair by the window. I think she was ninety years old at the time. This was to be my new home.

Before she gave us anything, she took us up to our bedroom and then along to another room where she undressed us and then proceeded to scrubs us down as if we were filthy dirty or had some horrible disease. I suppose the locals thought that all Londoners were dirty as they came from a dirty place but they could not have been more wrong. I should mention that she did this every day until I made her understand that she had no need to wash me, I was perfectly capable of doing this myself and I was very indignant being treated like a very little girl.

I don't remember having anything to eat or drink that night and when we were told to get undressed and then to go up to bed, I was mortified. Having to share a room with somebody else, even though it was only a little girl, was bad enough, but to get undressed in front of strangers was too much… I had only ever got undressed in front of my parents before this and now I was expected to do what I considered to be very nearly a public showing. I suppose I created a bit over this and that certainly didn't endear me to the two women.

Later, I lay in bed next to Valerie and felt very homesick. Although it had been a long day of excitement and travel, I could not go to sleep. I could feel Valerie sobbing beside me and that started me off. I don't know how long that went on for and eventually we both fell asleep. I do know that when we were crying in bed, no one came up to see what was the matter.

The next day I wanted to go out and explore the village and this was allowed. I went out and met some of the children who had come down with me and they were having a look around. The local people were looking at us from their open front doors and the local children were either with their parents or were down by the quay and the boats. I soon got used to finding my way about and I loved it down by the harbour and as it was a very hot summer, I loved to go in swimming.

I soon found out that life was going to be a lot different from what I had been used to, it was quieter for one thing and that was something that took a while to get acclimatised to, as I had lived in a street where there was a fair amount of traffic and we were near to Choumert Road market in Peckham. All that meant noise and I was used to it.

The local people regarded us children from London as something strange, cockneys we were called, they seemed to think that all Londoners were cockneys and could not understand when we explained that we came from south London, whilst true cockneys came from the East End.

Living with Mrs Howard introduced me to different types of food from what we normally ate in London. Mrs Howard, whatever else I might say about her, was a good

L to R:
Jessie Gardner;
Joan French;
Ruby Perry;
Dene Grice;
Ruth Cruse.

Man at Back Phil
Dunn

cook and she used to make potato pies and pasties. They were my favourites and I needed no urging to clear my plate. That was one thing about being in the country, all the fresh air and running about gave me a huge appetite and as she was a good cook, she satisfied my hunger. I remember all the fruit tarts she made, her pastry was terrific.

Mrs Howard was the village postmistress and she was also the Sunday School teacher in the little chapel that is in the back street behind her house. Of course this meant that we were expected to attend chapel every Sunday and after a few weeks of this, I opted out one Sunday but she made sure I was there and remained there throughout the service the following Sunday. She placed me in the front pew, right in front of her, so she could see what I was up to.

Every so often we had a guest preacher and he would have his Sunday dinner with us in Mrs Howard's house. Then we would have to be on our best behaviour and we were not allowed to play at all that Sunday. To me it became the worst day of the week.

The village school was at the top in the country part of the village and was only a small school, definitely not built to take in the hundred or so London children. It was a good thing that the weather was good that year, because our teachers took us for walks along the lanes, where we were taught not only nature but other lessons as well. Sometimes, to vary our walk, the teachers

Dene Grice on an outing to Bideford and all dressed up

would take us along the cliff tops or through the several woods in the village. On the few times that it rained, we went into a farmer's barn and had our lesson there. The walks in the countryside was the good part of it all as it was lovely, and gradually I grew to like Clovelly. If only my mother and father could have been with me, it would have been paradise.

When we did get into school, after several weeks of outdoor lessons without books or paper, we found that the main room, the hall was divided into three or four classes by hanging curtains across the room. There were two other classes in the other two rooms and the infants were sent to the old St.Peters chapel down in the village, where they were taught by another teacher.

The Head Teacher was Mr Hesketh, who was the local Head, and he was assisted by Miss Barbara Cruse. The teachers who came down with us were Mr Bamsey, Miss Plaice and Miss Woods. Mr Hesketh maintained very strict control over all of us and used the cane quite a lot, more it seemed, on the evacuee children than on the locals, but then, they were used to it in London and probably deserved it. I remember that one day, I was called out in front of the other children for something that I had done wrong, I forget now what it was, but Mr Hesketh caned me on my hands and although it hurt a lot, what really upset me was that it was done in front of all the others. I resolved to keep out of his way as much as possible after that.

When I think back to those days, when we all shared reading and text books on a one book between every two children, and were rationed to one writing book each year and used to scrounge paper of all colours and thickness to draw on, I wonder how we were ever educated. They moan nowadays about shortage of books but they cannot be as bad off as we were in 1940 – 41. I remember we used to have to write on the covers of the books when we had filled the pages.

The noise in the big room was bedlam at times. With only flimsy material as curtains between each learning group, you had to speak louder than the others to make yourself heard. If the next class were reciting their multiplication tables and you were taking dictation, it normally meant there were a lot of mistakes and if you had a reading lesson you had to nearly shout for the teacher to hear. The funny part came when you were still reading very loudly when the class next to you suddenly stopped reciting their tables. That usually produced laughter from some of the classes.

The school was heated by huge iron stoves that burnt coke and to prevent us getting ill from the fumes, they always had a bowl of water on top of each one. There were two stoves in the hall and one in each of the other rooms and to guard against the children getting burnt, there were high fire guards right around the stoves and fastened to the wall. I remember that when it rained, there always appeared to be a lot of wet clothes draped over the fire guards and soon learnt that these were the coats of the children who had walked two or three miles to school. There always seemed to be a crowd of children around the stoves on cold days, especially the wet or snowy days, that was during playtimes or dinner break.

Thinking of Wrinkleberry school has brought to my mind an incident in the lane that went past the school and down through the trees to the top of the cobbles. It is a very steep lane, very narrow, no more than six to seven feet wide, with high banks and hedges shutting it in. One winter there was lots of snow and it seemed that the children were sliding everywhere on sledges and I remember another evacuee, Ronnie Lomas, got hold of a sledge from somewhere and we were sliding about on it and having a good old time. We got to the steep part of Wrinkleberry Lane, and as it would be a good run, Ronnie let me have the go. What we had not taken into account was that where others had gone over the snow with their sledges, it had frozen over, so that the top of the snow was like ice. Anyway, I got on the sledge and Ronnie gave me a push to get me started and off I went. Faster and faster I went, in fact I was nearly flying, but I loved it until I saw that there was a sharp left hand bend ahead of me. It was an acute angle bend and it was coming up fast. There was no way I would be able to negotiate this bend and I would either hit the bank in a crash or go up over the bank and then down through the trees towards the roofs of the cottages below.

I don't really know whether I fell off or was thrown off the sledge, but I finished up skidding along the bank, doing the left hand turn on my own, with the sledge having sailed over the bank and smashed into a tree. There was not much snow on the bank and as I was moving along it face down, my chin was like a snow plough. It met sticks and stones and by the time I stopped, my face was hurting like the dickens. Ronnie came sliding down the lane, all concerned and when he saw me getting up from where I was lying, he started to laugh, that is until he saw the blood. Then he was worried and using his handkerchief and mine, he wiped the muck and blood away and found that I had a bad gash in my chin. I don;t remember going to see a nurse or a doctor about it and in time it healed up. I have a scar on my chin to this day which always reminds me of the snow in Wrinkleberry Lane and Ronnie Lomas.

I loved to walk in the woods and the fields in the Spring and the Summer, to see the birds, flowers and trees with their different leaves. One of my favourite places was the Hobby Drive, where you can walk along the private road through the trees and look out over the village; hundred or so feet below, and then out over the sea, across the bay. I know when we used to stop and look down on the roofs of the cottages, I often wondered if they could guess that some London kids were looking down on them from the Hobby. There were lots of other places that I walked but I cannot remember them now, and although I loved going to all these different places, I know now that I did not appreciate them as much as I do when I occasionally return with my husband these days.

As a child in Clovelly war often seemed a long way away, even though I was worried about my parents with the bombing and all that. I know that we used to have lessons about the war and we used to have gas-mask drills in the class, sometimes doing lessons whilst we were wearing the gas-mask. But the quietness and I suppose the distance from any form of war-like activity cossetted us. However, this was to be shattered one day when the war came to Clovelly.

I was playing with some friends in the Peace Park, which is at the top of the village, by the top of the cobbles, when a German plane came over and dived. We had been told many many times that if a plane dived at you, to throw yourself on the ground or get under cover. As we were beside the big trees, my friends and I ran under the branches at the same time as the plane started firing. I heard the bullets or whatever they were smashing through the tops of the trees above us. I remember we were petrified and as soon as the noise of the firing was over, we ran down into the village to be amongst other people.

Even though we were small, we knew that a German plane did not come over just to fire at little girls and frighten them. We guessed that it was trying to position himself to fire at the Royal Navy M.L. that was usually tied up at the lifeboat buoy, just off from the quay. Everyone was talking about it and some were saying that the M.L. had fired back at the German and that it had flown off with smoke coming out of it. I believe the lifeboat went out later and fished the pilot out of the water and brought him back to Clovelly.

My first Christmas in Clovelly was a sad time because I still missed my mother very much, more so as it was Christmas time. In my dark moments I wondered if I would ever see her again and when the war would end, so that I could go home. I remembered what it had been like in our home in Peckham, the excitement on waking up on Christmas morning, just like fairyland with all the presents. This first Christmas away from home was going to be so different.

I knew that my mother had sent me a present because just before Christmas, as I was going upstairs to my room, I saw two parcels lying under Mrs Howard's bed. To satisfy my curiosity I had to have a look, and saw that one was addressed to Valerie and one to me and that it was my mother's writing. We had the parcels on Christmas day and although it was exciting, it was not like waking up in your own home and bed and seeing the presents and pretty things in the room.

My father, who was a regular sailor in the Royal Navy, came home on leave and he and my mother came down to see me. They stayed at the Red Lion Hotel, down by the quay, and of course they had to have me with them as well. I thought it was great to be staying in the hotel with my mum and dad, and right beside the sea, on the beach in fact, so that when you looked out of the window, the sea was only a few feet away. Eating in the dining-room and being served by waitresses was a new experience for me and even though there was food rationing, there seemed to be plenty for us.

There was an occasion when a group of us boys and me – I was the only girl in the group – were walking along and exploring the beach. We had not realised how far we had walked or the state of the tide, I suppose because we were not used to such things, when we suddenly saw that the sea had reached the cliffs some way in front of us. As we knew we could not go on any further, we turned around to go back and saw that the sea had reached a point where the cliff jutted out farther than where we were standing. I got very frightened and I think the boys were as well, although some of them were trying to hide it. We couldn't go forward and we couldn't go back, so there was only one thing for it, go upwards.

We were very very fortunate to be in a position where it was possible to climb up, most places you cannot and people (tourists)are getting caught out every year and have to be rescued. But at that time, we knew nothing about such things and with a bit of help from one another, we scrambled up the cliff. In places there were holes you could put your toes in, sometimes there was a bush, which held our weight when we pulled on it to get up to another position.

Grazed knees and cut hands meant nothing to us in our desperation and we were determined to make it to the top. In between panting for breath and giving verbal encouragement to each other, we slowly made our way up to the line of trees. Once there, we knew that we should be safe. All we had to do then was to climb up the steep slope between the trees to reach the roadway of the Hobby Drive.

Eventually we got up to the trees and only occasionally stopping to rest against a tree, we kept going until we reached the roadway. Then we sat down and got our breath back. Looking at one another, I think we made a silent promise to each other not to mention this escapade to any one, but a look at ourselves and our clothes saw that some explanation would have to be given to our foster parents as our knees and hands were bloody, our clothes torn in places and marked with big red patches where we had come in contact with the beautiful red soil of Devon during our climb. I remember some of the names of the boys – Ronnie Lomas, Harry Littley and Russel Alexander. There were two others but I cannot remember their names. When I got home I was questioned as to what had happened and I told Mrs Howard the truth. I got a right telling off from her, not for climbing the cliffs, but for being out with the boys.

Mrs Howard was related to the Cruse family in the village and I got to make friends with them. There were girls as well as a boy. Most of the girls were older than me but the whole family were so friendly and I liked going there to see them and play with Ruth Cruse in her garden. Ruth had a brother named Tom and he was extra special but I won't say anymore about it. Now someone I shall never forget was Mrs Cruse, their mother. She used to give me a much needed cuddle every now and then which I loved and looked forward to. I suppose she was a natural mother with lots of love to give to others. They were very nice people and good to all the evacuees that used to call in to see them.

I well remember the Harvest Festivals in the chapel. Because I had no money to buy anything for the chapel, I used to go up to the woods and Hobby Drive and pick some wild flowers and twigs with the autumn leaves and then proudly carry them back for Mrs Howard to put in the chapel, they were my contribution. I used to think that the wild flowers were so lovely and delicate with beautiful colours, something that has never left me.

During the war, as there was petrol rationing, there were not many buses going from Clovelly, so we had to walk. We walked miles I suppose, when the weather was fine and thought nothing of walking three miles to the next village. I remember walking along the road to Bucks Mills, which is the next village along the coast, and as we walked I saw that there were loads of wild strawberries growing in the hedges. This was the first time I had seen so many growing and we had a lovely time picking and eating them, so much, that it took ages for us to get to Bucks Mills.

Clovelly is world famous for its cobbled High Street and the donkeys and when we were children in the village, it seemed that there were scores of donkeys, certainly a lot more than there are now. The donkeys were used to carry down the beer and other drinks to the New Inn Hotel and the supplies to the post office/shop in the High Street. Then they would be used again to carry up the empties, as well as the rubbish, in fact for most things because there were no motor vehicles allowed in the village. Donkeys were also an attraction for visitors and if a visitor was below a certain weight, they, mainly women, could ride up on the donkey for a shilling or two I believe. As children, we would walk up the High Street with whoever was handling a particular donkey or group of donkeys. As we would chatter away to them, they would get to know us and most people were friendly in the village, so after a while they would say, "D'you want to ride?" and of course we did. Thereafter, if the donkey was going up unladen, it was usually a ride for one of us. I have ridden down but I didn't like it. I seemed to be falling forward over the donkey's neck all of the time.

I have always thought that Clovelly was a wonderful place for children to play 'Hide and Seek'. We used to play it so often and if you were up at the top of the cobbles, you could either run down the High Street or cut through the Peace Park, which is very steep, and run through the alley that comes out at the 'Look Out', then down the winding cobbled street to the quay. There were dozens of places you could hide and they could never find you for ages.

In the summer, a lot of the evacuee children used to play and swim in the harbour and it was good fun, especially at week-ends or after we had finished school. I enjoyed it until I started to have trouble with my ears. I was in so much pain that Mrs Howard took me to the doctor, who called in at the village once a week. He examined my ear and told me that I must not swim again. That appeared to be that, but after the ear got better and the pain disappeared, I wanted to be with my friends again.

Well I was in the water with a friend, Barbara Bunce and another girl named Joyce. We had got undressed under a tarpaulin on a boat that was on the beach and then as the tide was in, we had a swim. Well, Joyce was showing off quite a bit with her swimming and jumping about doing acrobatics and that sort of thing when her costume came apart underneath. As the poor girl took hysterics, Babs and I went into fits of laughter. All the other children were looking now, because of the noise she was making and our laughing, and she then started yelling at us. She was furious with us, as if it was our fault. As she started to walk out of the water, the costume, no longer fastened between her legs, started to rise up to her waist. Trying to help, we threw her a towel which she missed and it fell into the water causing more screeches until Babs and I finally got her out of the water and back to the boat and left her under the tarpaulin to get dressed.

Some of the evacuee children that I remember at that time were Harry Littley, Alan Laundy, Ronnie Lomas, Harry Clement, Fatty Beasley, Barbara Bunce, Betty and Jill Gadd, Alan Davis, John Farley, Eileen Law, Billy and Ted Stapleton, Georgina Hunt, Eileen Ryan, Ray Lamb, Flossie Ellis, and Ruby Perry and her brother. Some of the local children were Katherine, Rachel, Faith, Ruth and Tom Cruse and Sheila Ellis.

I remember that the first time I had ever seen watercress growing was in a stream in the Hobby Drive. It looked like the stuff we used to buy in the greengrocers or in Choumert Road market in Peckham. So I scrambled across to the stream and picked a bit and put it in my mouth. It tasted the same so I picked a bit more and chewed it and it tasted good. I don't think we ever had it at Mrs Howard's.

There was a green gate at the top of the village that we used to go through, and there was a kind of field or park. I know that there were often animals in there and there was a footpath that went along the top of the cliffs. In this field in the Spring, there were lots of daffodils and primroses, trees in blossom and the sight and smell of them remains with me to this day. So much so, that when I left school at fourteen, I went to work in a florists so that I could be with flowers which I loved. I still occasionally make up basket arrangements and button-holes for friends or special dates.

I can remember a show being put on for us children at Clovelly Court and some of us took part. We dressed up in fancy dress and I was supposed to be a cook. Around the bottom of my apron were the words "Are we downhearted, NO! ". Across the middle of the apron were the amounts of a person's weekly rations, 2ozs. butter, 4ozs. tea, and sugar, bacon and things like that. Any proceeds were to go to the war effort. I had also rehearsed with some other girls a song entitled, "You can't come and play in our yard "but when it came for the big night I was too shy to go on.

The actor, Nosmo King was there with his son, Jack Watson, who is now a famous actor, and they were very well liked by everyone, especially the children, as they were so kind. It was a good night and I think everyone enjoyed it.

It was a shame, that although I was contented in Clovelly, and loved the countryside, and had many friends, I was not happy at the Howard's, and as time went by, things did not improve. I wrote a letter to my mother, telling her that I was unhappy and put in some home truths about Mrs Howard, but before my mother received the letter, Mrs Howard read it. There was a terrible fuss over it and she decided that I had to go. I was not given the option of being billeted with another Clovelly family, but sent to the evacuee hostel at the Rectory at Parkham.

Now just before I had written the letter to my mother, which started all the trouble, I had caught nits from someone or somewhere. Of course Mrs Howard did not know how to cope with it, thinking no doubt that I was dirty, but I wasn't. So when she read my letter, that was the last straw as far as she was concerned and out I had to go. I don't know where I got the nits but I remember that one Sunday I went to have tea with another evacuee, who was billeted on a farm and when I got back that night, I started scratching. They might have come from the animals but this is only my idea of how I might have caught them.

At Parkham there was a Matron in charge of the children and she was very strict with all of us and she got rid of my nits in no time at all with a special shampoo. I had only been there about one month when the head girl, as they called her, went home. The matron then made me head girl, and at the age of eleven I was making the children's beds, sometimes they would be wet, and getting three dormitories of children up, washed and dressed and ready for breakfast at nine o'clock.

I said that Matron was very strict, well she was and one of her punishments was to send to bed in the afternoons anyone that disobeyed her in a small way. I fell foul of her one day when we had apple pie for sweet and as I have never liked apple pie, I didn't eat it. This upset the Matron and after ordering me eat it several times and threatening me, she told me to go to my bed. It was not so bad in the winter I suppose, but when the weather was fine, it was a real punishment to lie in the bed and to hear the other children out in the garden.

Another thing I shall always remember her for was for her readings of the Bible. She would give each child some pages from the Bible to learn and then each child had to stand up in front of everyone and say the piece we had learned, woe betide any child that got it wrong.

I had always loved singing, and at Parkham, I was picked to sing in the choir. This gained me a few chalks I suppose and put me in Matron's good books – until next time. I liked singing in the church, or out of it and was at my happiest just singing. One thing being connected with the church at Parkham, the Rector there taught me how to play chess, so I learnt something after all in being sent to Parkham.

My mother joined the WRENS in 1941 and because she did not want to go away and leave me at Parkham, she decided, and I didn't object, to have me back and take me to stay with my grandmother in Peckham. So just before Christmas 1941, I returned to London.

We moved from Chadwick Road to a little further out to Barry Road, Peckham and because the bombing didn't seem to be any better there, we moved to Lewisham. Fate was against us for we were bombed out the first night that we had moved in. So back to Peckham and then to Forest Hill, which is about a mile or so down the road from our old house in Chadwick Road. In a short while, we were bombed out again. This time we were housed in my old school at Bellenden Road and we stayed there for three weeks with lots of other people who had been bombed out. As the school was only a short way from Chadwick Road, we moved back there and got a flat. The Germans were really trying for us because when the V1 and V2's started to hit London, we were hit again. This time the the house was not hit, the rocket was a near miss, but as they did so much damage, the blast hit us and the stairs disappeared and all ceilings came down.

I shall always remember the war years, as I went from the noise of London to the peace and beauty of Clovelly, then because of circumstances, back to an even noisier London. I was happy to be with my family again but if only I had stayed with someone like Mrs Cruse, who knows, I might have stayed there until the end of the war.

CHAPTER EIGHT

NETTLES, DANCING CLASSES AND JAUNDICE

My story encompasses all three items in the title of this chapter, and many more as well, and it is the memories that I have of those days in the early 1940's, when as Georgina Hunt, I left London as an evacuee to live in Clovelly in North Devon.

Thinking back to those days,I suppose if I had been old enough, I would have shared my parent's, Kate and George, concern for the state of the world in 1940. With the frightening rantings of Hitler and the march of German domination in Europe, it was no wonder that most adults had become extremely worried about German designs on Britain. I am told that there were many warnings from prominent people who spoke on the radio (wireless), also that the newspapers carried countless stories about the suffering of all who opposed Hitler and his gang.

Many years later, I talked with my parents about those days, about how they had coped, how they had decided to send my sister and I to be evacuated, the worries and fears that rested heavily upon all responsible parents, as the likelihood of German attacks on our towns and cities became more and more a certainty.

Home for me in 1940 was in the borough of Deptford, on the south bank of the River Thames and opposite to Millwall. Although only very young at the time, I well remember the docks and wharves that stretched along the river bank, with the vast Royal Victoria Victualling Yard lying in the centre of them all. You did not need to be a military strategist to realise that all the docks and wharves on the River Thames would be intended targets for the Luftwaffe when Hitler decided to send them over to London.

Although my father and mother saw the sense in evacuating children away from vulnerable places, they had reservations about official schemes where whole schools would be evacuated en masse. My father foresaw children arriving in their reception areas and being chosen for their looks and behaviour, merely at the whim of those intending to be the foster-parents. They discussed it at length, reviewing all the pros and cons, and I can only now realise the heartache they must have suffered in trying to reconcile their thoughts, and to do what was best for my sister Audrey and myself, who were only four and nine years old at the time.

My school was Clive Street School in Deptford and I am not sure to where the official school party were evacuated in 1940 but when my parents decided that Audrey and I should go, it was through another system, self help. Three doors away from us lived Mr and Mrs Thomas and their two children, who were our friends. Kenny and his sister Doreen had already been evacuated in June of 1940 to the village of Clovelly in North Devon and from what my parents understood, the family with whom Doreen was evacuated might be able to take my sister and I as well, that is, if we made our way to Clovelly under our own steam.

I forget exactly when we travelled to Clovelly, and thinking back, I suppose my mother must have written first and had a favourable answer from the family in question, Mr and Mrs Lenny Finch of West Dyke Farm. Anyway, we arrived at the farm and true to my father's theory, Mrs Finch liked the look of Audrey and myself and our behaviour and decided to take us in. She commented to my mother that she was pleased that my mother did not wear any make-up; viewing her no doubt from a solid rural church background that in the early 40's regarded the painting of women's faces as something only 'certain' women would do. My mother decided to let us stay with the Finch's, and many years later she said how my father was right in that we had been selected for our looks and behaviour.

Soon we were booked into the village school, called Wrinkleberry, although Audrey had to go down the cobbled High Street to an old chapel which in the emergency had been turned into a schoolroom for the younger children. From the farm we walked along the lanes, past the thatched shop and then to the main road leading through Higher Clovelly down to the village. As it was war-time, there was very little motorised traffic; the odd bus twice a day and maybe the butcher or baker. The rest of the traffic was horse drawn or cows being driven to or from the fields. Down Slerra Hill our route to school would go, right into Wrinkleberry Lane and at the end was a small hamlet of about five cottages and a farm.

Wrinkleberry School is now well over one hundred years old and like all village schools, is on one floor. A stone wall surrounds the school and it is bordered on two sides by fields which stretch all the way down to the woods lining the cliff edge and the top of Clovelly village.

To take Audrey to her class, I had to walk past Wrinkleberry school, along a narrow lane that led steeply down to where the main road, coming from a different direction, finished at the beginning of the famous cobbled street of Clovelly. Down the High Street, slipping and sliding on the cobbles, deposit Audrey at the chapel and climb all the way back up to the school. At the end of the afternoon session at school, this journey had to be repeated. I well remember rushing along in the mornings, with Audrey dawdling along behind, everytime I looked around to chivvy her into walking faster, she would cry, "I want my mummy, take me home." It upset me so much, it's a wonder I ever got to school at all.

I suppose certain instances stand out in one's mind more than regular routine happenings, and one I recall was when a certain boy evacuee pushed me into a some stinging nettles, shouting, "They don't sting this Sunday, only silly girls." I started to scream and he ran off leaving me to make my own way home, hurt and crying. Looking back, I can see it had just that touch of 'Just William' and 'Violet Elizabeth'. I have recently heard that Ray Lamb has confessed to being the culprit, but time heals and Ray is forgiven – until I find HIM conveniently near to a clump of nettles.

My mother used to come down to visit us whenever she could and I remember waving goodbye to her one snowy Sunday afternoon and then after she had gone, rushing into a snow covered field, crying and singing, "We'll meet again, don't know where, don't know when, etc." Even Vera Lynn would have been moved by the sight of that little London girl, standing in the middle of a wintery field, tears streaming down her face as she sang her song. That was my way to express my emotions as I could not do so openly in front of my mother, as I knew how sad and worried she was about us anyway.

The lady of the manor was Mrs Betty Asquith and she lived in the big house, Clovelly Court, which was surrounded by grounds and parkland. Mrs Asquith had several horses and polo ponies and these were often exercised by her daughter Christine, a good looking girl with long fair hair who was in her late teens. There were quite a lot of Deptford boys billeted at Clovelly Court and one of these was Kenny Thomas, so after a while I got to know Christine and I started to learn to ride with her. She was so friendly and had so much patience with me, in fact her kindness made the separation from home so much easier to bear.

Wrinkleberry school was so crowded with children; built to hold possibly forty pupils, it had, during my stay, about 250 to 300 children, mostly evacuees from Peckham, Deptford, Bristol and Plymouth. The head teacher was Mr Hesketh, who was very strict, some teachers from London, one lady teacher from Plymouth and one local lady teacher who taught the infants. As there were only three rooms in the school into which some five or six classes of pupils had to be fitted, the authorities divided the large room (hall) with two or three large curtains across the room, making some three or four 'classrooms'.

Just imagine the din, the absolute bedlam when classes were in the midst of their lessons. Multiplication tables being recited whilst others behind the curtain might be doing dictation or reading poetry, teachers raising their voices to be heard above the noise and tempers often becoming manifest, resulting in instant punishment. Under those circumstances it is no wonder that the cane, the slap around the ear, or the crash of a blackboard scrubber exploding on the side of the head, were often the weapons with which the teachers kept some form of discipline; but it did little for the peace and stability required for learning. That being said, it was war-time with terrible conditions everywhere and the authorities had a tremendously hard job on their hands and they coped well.

There were two ladies in Clovelly who were I believe friends of Mrs Asquith and somehow they gathered several girls together, mostly evacuees, and obtained some premises from Mrs Asquith for their project. Miss Woodall and Miss Scott were intent on teaching the girls to dance and to do skipping exercises to music, so as to make a show of it and soon we were attending every Saturday morning in a room above the stables at Clovelly Court. One would teach us the steps and coach us, whilst the other worked the gramophone, I can see her now, furiously winding the gramophone to keep the music at the right speed. I think there were one or two different classes because of the ages, some girls being no more than six whilst others were twelve or thirteen. They were certainly very kind ladies who gave a lot of their time to we girls, who perhaps were not the best material with which they hoped would be a dance troupe.

Sometimes on Sundays I would enjoy some wonderful happy hours when some other children would come up to West Dyke and play with me. That being said, I should mention that Sundays were always very busy for me for I had to go to church in the morning, followed by Sunday school in the afternoon and then church in the evening. It appeared that Mrs Finch was a very regular church goer and expected the same from her charges.

My memories of Mr and Mrs Finch at West Dyke Farm are that Mrs Finch was kind but severe, Mr Finch was so extremely warm hearted with a great sense of fun, so much so, that he was like an older brother. They both seemed to work so very hard over long hours and never complained about it in our presence. Mrs Finch would have her housework and cooking to do as well as several tasks about the farm. Mr Finch was in the Home Guard and often when he was cleaning his gun, he would let me help him clean it, it was his pride and joy. He would talk to me like an adult and say, "We'll get the b . . . . . .s", referring to the Germans, "if they try anything on." He was also my first political guru and some of his saying remained with me, "We will have to watch those Chinese after the war, and the Russians will not always be ours friends." It was often well above my head and comprehension but I liked being in his company as he cheered me up and made me laugh a lot, also I learned a lot from him. When Mrs Finch was being a bit careful over the rations, he would later beckon me into the pantry and give me an extra portion, saying, "We little 'uns use up a lot of energy."

Often during the long winter evenings, Mr and Mrs Finch would have a musical evening, he playing the violin and she the piano. I had very musical parents and so was used to lots of entertaining at home, so I looked forward to these occasions very much.

Mr Finch taught me how to drive a horse in a cart and I would often go out with him to fetch in a load of turnips or mangelwurzels, sitting up on the two-wheeled cart and driving the horse. One day however, I learnt something else because as I was coming out of the field, my horse either tripped over or slipped on a wurzel, and the outcome was that the cart tipped over, I jumped clear, the

Raymond Wills; Mrs. Westlake; Mary Westlake; Bobby Couchman. 1942

96

load came out and one of the shafts broke off. I expected Mr Finch to be flaming angry over the broken cart but once he had got the horse free and discovered that I was not hurt, he just seemed to shrug it all off as one of those things. I no longer thought of myself as an expert horse driver, which was a good lesson to learn.

I suffered a series of personal mishaps during my stay in Clovelly and Mr and Mrs Finch coped and nursed me through them all. I developed yellow jaundice on one occasion and that freed me from attending school for a while; how I got it or from where I really don't know. On another occasion, whilst playing at school a tree trunk fell on my head. On reflection, I must have climbed over the school wall, dropped into the field and run down to the woods with so many other children to play. I came out of that scrape with a slightly split head and a headache. Once more my guardian angel stepped in and saved me when one day,whilst out with Christine Asquith and others, learning to ride properly, for some reason or another, my horse bolted with me perched not too confidently on its back. Luckily the horse kept to the path through the woods and I stayed, albeit a little untidily, in the saddle until eventually the horse decided that it had obtained sufficient satisfaction in revenge for the unskilful mishandling of its rider and he came to a halt. You can imagine the scene, my horse in the lead, galloping along the path through the woods with Christine and the other in full cry behind me. No doubt poor Christine was wondering what on earth the horse would do when it arrived on the stoney beach of Mouth Mill, which was in the direction I or rather my horse was heading. I suffered little more than a sore backside and hurt pride, especially as it had all occurred in front of some of the other evacuees.

The authorities had converted the Rectory coach-house into a canteen to provide mid-day meals for the evacuees; I suppose to relieve the burden of rationing that the foster parents had to bear. It appeared that droves of children turned up every day for their lunch, which was always very substantial, pies, meat puddings etc. and plenty of vegetables followed by large helpings of apple pie and custard or whatever fruit was in season and custard or milk puddings. Of course some of the boys would always go back for 'seconds'. After the meal there was the long climb back to school and some took the back way up the steep narrow Wrinkleberry Lane, others would walk around by the main road whilst many of the boys would climb over gates and hedges and cut across the fields to the gate opposite the school. In wet weather, those that arrived back at school having travelled via the back lane or cut across the fields, could always be identified by the red Devon mud on their shoes and boots, and if they had slipped, as many regularly did, then they would also have it on their clothes. It was to this canteen that the girls had to go for cookery lessons and the general house work expected of women in those days, but it did me no harm at all, in fact it has all stood me in good stead over the years.

In the warm weather, a lot of us London children used to flock down to the harbour and the beach, for us it was paradise, the seaside right on our very own doorstep. Now living in the village for the duration of the war was a gentleman and his wife, by the name of Mr and Mrs Watson. He was a radio personality using the name Nosmo King and was very well known at the time, frequently appearing on the popular Saturday night programme, 'In Town Tonight'. Often he would be down at the harbour or sitting on the beach and he was a great favourite with the children, for whom he appeared to have an immense amount of patience. One day he was sitting on the beach with us and he was making up poems, using our names and when it came for my turn, I was very disappointed that he could not think of anything rhyming with Georgina. However he made me a promise and later he fulfilled that promise by letting me sing and dance in a concert that he produced with his son Jack. He told me afterwards that this was far more important than a poem.

If seeing me on the stage was a surprise to many of the children, it was certainly no surprise to Kenny Thomas. Back home in Deptford, I would often dress up in my mother;s clothes and put on concerts in the back garden for the other children. Kenny was the only one who never ran away once he had had the biscuits and lemonade that my mother provided at the interval. Seeing that I was trying to impersonate Jessie Matthews, Shirley Temple and Marlene Deitrich it was a wonder that he came at all. We were very good friends as children and sadly we only met once after the war, when we stood on the bomb site of what once had been our houses and talked about the war-time years. I was very sad to hear years later that Kenny had died relatively young.

There came the time when the heavy raids on London had eased somewhat and my mother wanted us with her, but no doubt listening to the cautionary words from my father, she resisted the temptation of taking us away from Clovelly. Nevertheless, she wanted to be with us and eventually it was agreed that she would come down and stay at West Dyke Farm with us, at least until the raids had stopped completely. Now we had our mother with us and we felt nearly like a family again.

She soon got on very well with Mr and Mrs Finch   helping around the house and looking after us. She used to get up early in the mornings to light the fire and get the place warmed up in time for when they started work and had breakfast. Her stews and roasts were popular and Mrs Finch told my mother that she was surprised of mother's capabilities as she was so small; I suppose there was so much that they could learn from each other. At times, mother and Mr Finch would share a cigarette, something in ordinary times they might never have done, but as cigarettes were scarce, it was becoming an accepted practise among friends and it proved how well Mr Finch and mother got on together.

An incident which I will never forget was when my mother and several other ladies were invited to attend a garden party at Court House. A lot of fuss was made about a particular tin container which read 'Cadbury's Chocolates' and this was to be the star prize of this charity raffle. As chocolates were in such short supply and never seen on the shelves of shops, it was something they all wanted to win. When the time came for calling out the numbers, my mother found to her delight that she had won the top prize and after receiving it from Mrs Asquith could hardly wait to get back to her chair to open the box. All excited she lifted the lid, with many ladies looking on, no doubt hoping for at least one chocolate, when to my mother's amazement, the tin was found to be empty. Not knowing whether to laugh or cry, my mother contained herself and with gracious disdain announced, "Please re-raffle it. Your need is greater than mine." When we arrived back at the farm mother talked it over with Mr and Mrs Finch and they just could not fathom out the mystery of the missing chocolates, especially as the box had been donated by the two Miss Cadbury who were living in Clovelly at the time. As these two ladies had approached my mother about letting me stay with them for the duration, Mr Finch's remark was particularly apt and made us fall about laughing when he said, "I think you'd better take up their offer and then ask them to fill the box."

I don't know when it was that I was told that my home in Deptford had been blown to smithereens along with the rest of the street and that when my sister and I eventually returned, it would not be to the same area. Consequently when the time came in early 1943 for us to leave West Dyke, after saying farewells to our friends and the Finches, my mother brought Audrey and myself to our new home at Canvey Island.

I can't say that my evacuation was particularly happy. I had come from a very loving and cossetted background with plenty of everything and I was not prepared for the Spartan lifestyle. However I did learn to milk a cow, ride a horse and drive a tractor and it became a subject of amusement when I married my own farmer. What the evacuation really taught me though was not everyone was as privileged as myself and also how kind complete strangers can be to one another. This feeling has stayed with me always.

CHAPTER NINE

EATING, SINGING AND HORSES

My name is Raymond Wills and this is my story.

In 1941, I was 12 years old and my mother had just died. I was living at home with my father and the Germans were bombing Bristol pretty badly, especially down by the docks, although it seemed that there was damage everywhere. There was a lot of talk going around at school that the authorities might be sending children out of Bristol to live in the countryside to escape the bombing.

As these stories were more or less being confirmed, my mind centered on thoughts of the country. All I could think of were horses and other animals and no school. This seemed to me to be an ideal situation so I told my dad that I wanted to go and after a while he answered to the effect that if that was what I wanted, then I could go. At least I should be safe in the country.

Like a good many families in those days, we did not have much in the way of luggage, so my dad's old army kitbag from the 1914-1918 war, was brought into use again. When the day of departure came, and I can remember the exact day, it was the 19 February 1941, my big sister came to see me off and I strode along the pavement with my gas mask slung around my neck, a name tag tied with string to my jacket lapel and my dad's kitbag over my shoulder. I felt like a soldier going to war but I was only going as far as the school. There I found that they had a line of double-decker buses waiting for us and as our names were called out, so we got on the bus.

You can imagine the chaos on the bus. names were being called out without reference to friends that wished to sit together or to the bulky weight of the bags, parcels, suitcases or kitbags that children had to handle. There was me, assigned to the top deck and trying to drag dad's kitbag up the stairs behind me, with another child behind being reprimanded by the teachers for not getting a move on.

We all started to sing the songs that were popular then, the Services songs I suppose, and one of them was, "Wish me luck as you wave me goodbye". All the mothers were crying and waving and shouting, "Be a good boy "or "Look after your sister and don't get split up" and then the buses started off.

For most of us children, especially the older ones, it was a great adventure. Some of the smaller ones were having a weep and being comforted by their brothers or sisters and some of the teachers. To them at that time, the countryside meant nothing, all they knew was that they were being taken away from their parents, their home and all that made up their little world.

When we arrived at Bedminster Railway Station, we were told to get off the buses and line up. Again confusion and chaos but eventually we were led onto the platform and found a train already there and waiting for us. Somehow or other, there were some parents on the platform and again there was the crying and shouting of instructions to the particular children. With a blast on its whistle, the train pulled away. Countryside here we come.

As we travelled along, a lady on the train came to tell us they we were going to the prettiest village in Devon, named Clovelly. Neither meant very much to us at the time, but I remember that after a while, the train passed close to the sea and we could all see the water, the sand and boats upon the beach. I can clearly recall that we were very excited and that I told the other children that we would come back later and play. I subsequently found out that this place was Instow.

Shortly afterwards, we arrived at Bideford Railway Station and there were more double-decker buses for us. On we got with the same confusion as before, and were taken across the bridge to a hall to be fed. The meal over, back on the buses again and off we went to Clovelly. I remember the sky coming over all dark and then it started to snow. Eventually we arrived at Clovelly Court and the end of our journey we thought. Here we were to be allocated to our foster homes (billets) but as we stood there in lines, tired and on show whilst people came up to look at us, then read the details on our name tag, all that most of us wanted was to get into a warm bed.

After a while it seemed that all the children had been chosen except my friend and I and then a big man told us to follow him. We got to a little van and he told us to put our things in the back and get in. He drove off, up the very steep hill that later I was to get to know so very well, and then we stopped outside a white cottage that was next to the village post office. My friend was told that this was his billet and to fetch his belongings with him and to follow the man into the cottage.

By now it was very nearly dark and we drove off again. Up and down hills, through lanes and I was wondering where on earth I was going, After a while we stopped again and as I got out I saw that we were outside three cottages and one was painted white. The man said that this was my billet. With my kitbag over my shoulder, I went through the little green gate, up to the door, on which the man knocked and the lady who answered it asked us inside. This was to be my new home and at first glance, it appeared that it might be a happy one.

I went and sat on the sofa and saw that there was a lovely fire burning in the grate, the lady had a flowery apron on and there were two children, one a boy the other a girl, reading comics. After the man, who had brought me, had gone, the lady, who was standing by the table, asked if I would like a boiled egg, when I replied that I would, she went on to ask me if I liked brussels sprouts, turnips, cabbages. I told that I didn't like any vegetables or hot dinners but preferred fancy cakes instead. She told me that I would have to get to like them as I would be having plenty of them if I stayed with her. How right she was. Soon she had me sat at the table having my tea. The time was five-thirty.

Shortly afterwards, about six o'clock, I heard the sound of the gate being opened and a bike being wheeled up the path. The back door opened and a man came into the house where he was greeted by the woman and the children. He came up to me and shook hands and said that if I was a good boy and behaved myself, I would have a good home with them. How right he was; I couldn't have wished to be better treated or fed.

Round about eight o'clock I went into the scullery and was shown how to use the water pump on the wall to get water to wash. Having washed and cleaned my teeth, I changed into my pyjamas and with the other boy was taken up to our bedroom. We were to share a bed and I discovered that he was also an evacuee, but from London. That day marked for me the end of my city life and the start of my country life, at least until the war was over.

MY FIRST MORNING

When I woke up the next morning, the only sounds that I heard were the crows squawking in the trees nearby. No other sounds came to me and that was strange for a city boy to understand. No noise of trams, cars, lorries and buses, people talking as the walked along the pavements to work.   Just about then, the lady called up the stairs for us to get up and dressed as breakfast was ready. Down we went, washed ourselves and had breakfast. I found out that the people I was billeted with were Mr and Mrs Westlake and their daughter Mary, who was seven years old, the same age as the Peckham evacuee.

Later that morning we all walked together when Mrs Westlake set out to visit her mother-in-law. Mrs Westlake wheeled her bike and gave each of us children turns to ride on it as she pushed it along. We visited a cottage at Turnpike in Higher Clovelly and I discovered that it was the same white cottage that my friend was billeted in the night before, when the man with the van was taking us around.

The home of the Westlakes was on the main Hartland to Bideford Road and was just about on the edge of the parish boundary between Hartland and Clovelly and the cottage was in Clovelly parish. It was called Southdown Cottage and there was a farm down the lane called Southdown Farm. My new home had a small front garden and a large back garden with wonderful views of the sea across the low lying fields between. Later on I used to stand in the garden and watch the convoys of ships going past, some with barrage balloons flying above them.

One thing that I found hard to get used to was the toilet. This was way up at the top of the back garden and was really just a little stone shed with a door and with a wooden seat with a hole cut in it. I soon discovered that it was not a flush toilet and that there was some sort of container beneath. There was always a smell of Jeyes Fluid about the place and a can of it was always kept in the toilet.

In his spare time, Mr Westlake worked hard in his garden, growing most of the fruit and vegetables that we ate in the home. I remember he grew All the Year Round

Greens, beans, peas, root crops, onions, gooseberries, blackcurrants and rhubarb. Our close neighbours in the other cottages, butchers, and the farms were Mr & Mrs Prowse who had two Bristol evacuees called Peter Smith and John Hudson; Mr & Mrs Johns; Mr & Mrs Cruse, the butcher and their house was called The Retreat; Mr & Mrs Slee at Highford Farm; Mr & Mrs Symonds at Southdown Farm and Mr & Mrs Cordray.

After I had been at my new home for about one week, Jeff Symonds from Southdown Farm, rode up one day on his way home from school. He told me that I had to be at school the next Monday. I asked him what school did he mean and he replied that I had to go to Clovelly school.

Monday came and after breakfast off we set, a whole bunch of us as it transpired. There was Mary, Bob and myself from Southdown Cottage; Jeff Symonds with two evacuees,the Carter brothers from Southdown Farm; Jean Goulding, Jill Gadd and Pat Reid, three London evacuees from London and who were living at The Retreat, together with Miss Barbara Cruse, who taught at the school. Ten of us in one bunch going off to school and our route, which I was to get to know so well, explained something of my journey in the van on my arrival the week before. What had appeared to me to be a mysterious winding way, now became clear. Along the main road from Southdown, up Providence Hill, left into Westdyke Lane, past the farm, Hugglepit Cross to Turnpike. Left down Slerra Hill and right into Wrinkleberry Lane and down at the end was the village school.

The school was packed with children as there were over two hundred evacuees from London and Bristol as well as the local children, so the noise – until order was restored – was terrific.   I found that there were some teachers from London as well as Mr Baker who came down with us from Bristol. Mr Hesketh was the Headmaster and Miss Cruse taught the infants. All this in a school which I suppose was only meant to hold thirty or so pupils.

I seem to remember that Mr Hesketh was only lodging in Clovelly, his home was in Axminster, South Devon, where he had been teaching prior to coming to Clovelly. Mr Bamsey, from London was lodging in Higher Clovelly, Miss Plaice from London was lodging at London Lodge in Higher Clovelly and Miss Wood from London, was I believe, staying somewhere down in the village.

This was to be the start of my country schooling.

DAD'S VISIT TO CLOVELLY

I suppose because he lived near me and we were about the same age that Jeff Symonds and myself became friends. One day in April he called for me and I saw that he had his pony tied by the gate. He asked Mrs Westlake if I could go with him to the blacksmiths, so off we went, taking it in turns to ride the pony along the road. By now I knew the road, as I passed the blacksmith's shop every day when I went to school. I got to know a lot of the local men and women as we passed in the lanes, or walked past their cottages and farms. The blacksmith was Mr Gist and he worked with his two sons and they did all types of ironwork and often I used to stop on my way home from school and watch them at work.

Anyway, the pony was shoed and Jeff and I were going up the road towards Turnpike, when I saw my dad standing outside Grandma Westlakes white cottage. He had his trilby hat on and was holding his case. I ran like mad to him and we greeted each other and he told me that he had arrived in Bideford late on Saturday night. He had been told that there was no transport to Clovelly until Monday so he had to stay in town. He had asked a policeman where he could find lodgings and had only just got to Clovelly now, on Monday morning. I've just thought, as we were not at school it must have been some kind of holiday, maybe Easter Monday.

My dad had just got off the bus and was wondering how to find out where I was living. So off we all went together, Jeff, my dad and myself, walking along the lanes and out onto the main Hartland Road, down Providence Hill to Southdown Cottage. I had already pointed it out to him from a distance, but it only looked as big as a dolls house then and now we were outside the gate.

Mrs Westlake was out in the back garden, hanging out the washing and I introduced her to my dad and she said that he should have let her know that he was coming down. Whatever her thoughts on the matter, she soon had us sitting down to a meal.

As we sat in the kitchen after the meal, my dad asked if there was anywhere we could go and I suggested that we walk down to Clovelly village. I knew he had never seen anywhere like it before and that it would be a nice surprise for him.

Off we set, walking back along the same road back to Clovelly again, past the blacksmith's, past the school and down to the cobbles. It had started to rain as we walked along and when we got to the top of the cobbles, dad looked down the High Street and asked if we had to walk all the way down. I told him we had to to see the place. He was fascinated with the houses and wondered who had built them all on the side of the hill. Anyway, dad made it to the bottom and we walked along the quay and looked out to sea, then up at the village perched on the side of the cliff. He took me into the Red Lion Hotel, by the quay and we had a nice tea with plenty of cakes. After we had finished, he said to me, "I want you to stay and stick it out down here Ray, you are far better off here than back with the bombs." He added that it should be more beautiful when the summer came.

Dad might have had misgivings about walking down the cobbles, now we were going home to Southdown, he had to walk all the way up again. Back we went, up to the top of the cobbles, up the lane past the school, up Slerra, Turnpike, Westdyke Farm and down Providence Hill. We were feeling hungry and tired when we reached Southdown Cottage and we could smell baking and cooking drifting out of the house. When Mr Westlake came home, we all sat down to a lovely meal and Mrs Westlake said she had arranged for Bob Couchman, the other evacuee, to move next door to Mrs Prowse's, so that my dad could sleep with me.

Because my dad was there, I stayed up a little bit longer than normal and my dad came to bed a lot later. I could hear him and the Westlakes downstairs, laughing and talking for ages. I think they liked my dad because he was jolly and he was always telling stories with a great sense of humour. My dad left the next morning by the eleven o'clock bus to Bideford. We all knew why he had come down, he had to see where I had been placed to live out the war. He left happy because he knew I was in good hands. He never came again; I think it was all that walking.

MY COUNTRY SCHOOL

I well remember the school at Clovelly, it was called Wrinkleberry because the hamlet of three cottages and the two farms were called Wrinkleberry. It was a typical village school, single storeyed, with two rooms and one larger one that could be called the hall. It was a mixed school for both girls and boys from five years until they left school at fourteen.

Mr Hesketh was the Head-master and I can see him now in my mind's eye, whenever he was addressing us on something he wished to emphasise, he would pull a

Raymond Wills 1942

chair close to where he was standing and put one foot up on the chair. I recall that he was very firm but fair. Whenever he was taking us to play cricket on the Lawn at Clovelly Court or to go gardening, he would wear his sweater slung around his shoulders, with the sleeves tied across his throat. He always enjoyed his sport and encouraged us to take part in as much as our other studies and war-work allowed us. He introduced us to Shinty and obtained the sticks from somewhere and we used to play that either on the cinders in the car-park or on the Lawn.

Mr Bamsey used to take us older boys and girls for history. He would hang a map over the blackboard and then point at various places and get us to tell him where it was. We could not see the print on the map, so we had to know where he was pointing. After a while, he would put a map up to show us how the war was going and we would talk about different places and their importance.

Singing lessons were something that I enjoyed more than anything else and I used to look forward to them every week. As I had a good voice, the teacher would get me to stand in front of the class and sing, sometimes it would be 'Land of my Fathers'; 'Drink to me only with thine eyes'; or 'Early one morning', then the class would join in with the chorus.

The school caretaker was Mrs Pengilly, who lived in a thatched cottage across the lane from the school. She would clean the school, wearing a long black apron, and in the winter carry buckets of coke and place them beside the big cast iron stoves in the hall, light the stoves and get the place warm before school… There was always a huge pile of coke in the playground at the back of the school, near to the boys toilets.

Around the stoves were high steel fireguards (railings) and those children that had to walk a long way to school and some walked about two and a half miles, could hang their coats over them when they arrived at school, so they could dry out. I remember being in class and seeing clouds of steam coming off the coats. On the top of each stove was a pan of water to absorb some of the fumes from the coke and in the winter, those children who had brought pies or pasties for lunch, could place them on the back part of the stove about an hour before lunch time, so that they would be hot to eat.

Some of the evacuees went down to the Rectory canteen for their lunch and as most of the boys were engaged in 'Digging for Victory' on two large plots of land that were granted to the school, we grew much of the food that was eaten in the canteen. One of the plots, named Wonnacott's, was about a quarter of an acre in size and was nearly opposite East Dyke Farm, about one mile from school, and when we took it over, it was a complete mess. If it had ever been a garden it must have been over a hundred years before. We had to cut down the brambles and long weeds and then with the spades and forks provided by the school, dig the turf over in the Winter and hope it would rot down a bit before the Spring. For many of us, it was the first time we had ever done any gardening and as we knew nothing about it, Mr Hesketh taught us. We did well and starting in the Summer of 1941, we were supplying the canteen with salads and vegetables.

I remember that we grew a lot of spinach and Mr Hesketh told me I could take some home, so I filled my satchel with it and when it was later cooked at home, it hardly filled an egg-cup.

The other plot of ground that we boys cultivated was down Wrinkleberry Lane, between the school and the top of the cobbles. It was an old well established garden with lots of fruits trees and bushes from which we got plenty of apples, pears, gooseberries and currants in their season. There was also a fair size bit of ground to dig in which we planted the usual salad and green crops. When I think back on all that we grew, it is easy to see how we kept the canteen supplied. I know that some of us would pick the apples and pears and shove them up our jerseys to hide them from Mr Hesketh and then later give them to the girls.

At dinner time we would cut across the fields as a short cut to the canteen, eat our meal and if any child didn't want their 'afters', we would ask for it, gobble in down then run all the way back across the fields to school again.

Every week if it was fine, we would sit out in the playground and thread green braiding through a big net. They told us we were making camouflage netting for the army. Other war work that we did was collecting waste paper from all the houses and farms. We would go miles for this, even when it snowed and then instead of a cart we took sledges. All the paper was taken back to the school and weighed and tied in bundles until someone collected it in a lorry. There were prizes for the school that collected the most in any week,but as far as I know, Clovelly never won anything.

Mr Hesketh lodged at the blacksmith's, Mr and Mrs Gist and at week-ends he would go home to his wife in Axminster. I remember he had a little grey Austin Seven that he would use on these trips and on Fridays we would see him start off. Sometimes the car wouldn't start and he would get some of the boys to give him a push to start it. He always seemed to have sweets on a Friday and he would give us some before he went.

These were the days when very few people had water in their homes and those that did, had only a small pump fitted over the sink. Mostly the pump was on the side of the road and first thing in the mornings would be the time to see the ladies carrying the water back to their homes. It might take several journeys before they had sufficient for their needs.

Mr Squires was the carrier and he used to go to Bideford every day and bring back all sorts of things that people needed, sometimes we kids would get a ride with him.

Some of the children really took to country life, even to wearing clothes like the locals. I remember one Bristol evacuee called Ginger Cable, he started to wear corduroy breeches, gaiters and big hob-nailed boots, a lot different from when he first came down to Clovelly.

LEARNING ABOUT HORSES

I was one of those that loved the slow country life and I would mix in with what the local boys were doing as often as I could. One day, Brian Slee, one of the sons of the neighbouring farmer at Highford Farm, called to ask me if I would like to go with him to take the horse to be shod. He had a huge horse with him that his father had just bought, it was called Lion and was seventeen hands high. It was a farm horse and of course didn't have a saddle, just a sack thrown over his back.

Well, off we went, taking it in turns to ride and to mount, we had to take it to a hedge to climb on. The horse got shoed and we were on our way back and had just reached the top of Providence Hill, I was just trying to get on the horse and was halfway across its back when two fighter planes came over very low. The horse reared, bolted down the road with me lying across its back, the sack slipped and off I went. As I lay in the road, all I could hear was the sound of the new shoes ringing out. We got a lift in a lorry and when we got to the bottom of the hill, Brian's father was there holding the horse, which was sweating and trembling. He was working in the field and had heard the horse galloping down the road and came out and stopped it. I seem to remember that he gave us words of advice.

Another horse riding incident that comes to my mind was when Jeff Symonds decided after Sunday School one sunny afternoon that a group of us could take it in turns to ride his pony in the field. After a while he decided to bring his pony out on to the road. There was very little traffic about in those days and we took it in turns to ride. When it was my turn, I jogged along for about a hundred yards outside the chapel, turned and just touched the pony with my heels. Well it was just like being shot out of a gun. I talked to the pony to get it to stop, I shouted and pulled at the reins but to no avail, it kept going. As we passed the group of children on the side of the road, they were all cheering just like a rodeo and the pony and I flashed by. Thankfully it stopped a few hundred yards up the road and I quickly jumped off before it changed its mind. It was a different Raymond Wills that returned leading the pony, although I made out the pony was doing what I wanted.

Another incident involving horses was again with Jeff, when one day, Mary, Bob and myself went down to Southdown farm to play in the barns with Jeff. Mr Symonds came out and told Jeff to take the horse cart down to a field and collect some mangolds. Mary, Bob and myself with Jeff's little brother, jumped up into the two-wheeled cart and Jeff drove off. The field was on a steep slope and part way up the field we all got out and started pulling the mangolds. When we had filled it, we all got back on and as Jeff started to drive off and was making a turn to go back home, the cart turned over, throwing us and the mangolds out. The poor horse was trapped in the shafts and lying on his side, trying to get up but couldn't. One of the shafts snapped and Jeff was trying to unharness the horse and I ran over to shout to a man in the next field. He came over and got the horse out and we were relieved to find that it was all right. When we got back to the farm Jeff got a lecture from his dad and we stayed away from Southdown for a bit.

MY WEEK-END WALKS

Every Saturday morning I used to walk into Hartland, which was about two miles from the cottage. I used to go in for groceries which I would put in the satchel over my shoulder. Usually it was the 'rations', yeast, cotton, cigarette papers and tobacco for Mr Westlake and there would always be some footwear for repair. Mr Tom Prowse, the cobbler, and I hit it off straight away and he would call me Bristol. When I called at his shop, I remember that the bell would ring everytime the door was opened and I would call out "Tom!" and he would call back, "Is that you Bristol." When I answered he would tell me to come up and I would climb the few stairs to his workshop at the back. I used to marvel at him sitting there with his mouth full of tacks as he hammered away at someone's boot or shoe. I would normally stay chatting to him for about half an hour as he worked and he knew I liked having steel shoes on the heels of my boots and plenty of steel studs on the soles. He never charged me much and said that he wanted me to work for him when I left school and he would teach me the trade.

I loved walking to Hartland and also the walk back if the weather was fine, which is all that we remember really. Sometimes I would leave the main road and go by the back lanes, past old ruined stone barns and hardly ever saw a soul. I would stop by field gates and look over at the corn or grass, at times look at the rabbits feeding or lying down in the sun. In those days you could usually hear someone working with horses in the fields, as you heard the instructions shouted to the horse. Then I walked on over the little stone bridge, out of the lane and onto the road near the cottage. Everything was so peaceful with a feeling of contentment, yet there was a war on and all around people were being killed.

SUNDAYS

On Sunday mornings I would go to Providence Methodist Chapel, which was just along the road from the cottage, for morning service. In the afternoons we children would go to Sunday School in the same chapel but up the stone steps into a little room at the back, where Mr Andrew Cory, Mr Slee, Mary Cory and Marjorie Slee would teach the little ones about Jesus and the older children would have Bible class. The preachers were usually lay-preachers and they came from around the district to Providence.

The Cruse family from The Retreat also came to chapel and I remember Mrs Cruse well, she used to wear big brimmed hats that reminded me of the lady at the start of Gainsborough films in the cinema. Mr Cory would come to chapel with his daughter Mary, in a big Ford motor car. It was always so polished you could see yourself in it and I remember it had a roof that used to go back to convert into an open tourer. It had a big horn on it with a great big rubber bulb and you could often hear him coming, just by the sound of the horn.

Harvest Festival was always a nice time in the chapel with the sheaves of corn laid at the front with all different kinds of garden and field produce. Everyone wore their best clothes and the chapel would be full. We children had a text to say with each child reading out a verse; it was called 'You may telephone Him from here', which was about being in God's House and bringing your troubles to Him. Once I sang a hymn by myself called, "In our dear Lord's garden planted here below, many tiny flowerets in sweet beauty grow." The caretakers at one time were Mr and Mrs Cordray and their son. They kept the chapel spotless and you could always smell the polish. The pews and floor were always shiny, with the vases full of flowers in season. They lived in accommodation at the back of the chapel and I remember the son kept a lot of hens and sold eggs to the Ministry of Food.

OUR TINKER

The cat belonging to Mr and Mrs Cordray at the chapel, had kittens and they gave one to Mary, my Mrs Westlake's daughter. It was black with white chest and paws. As it grew up, like most country cats, it took a liking for rabbits in the fields and was always catching them for food. It was always a comical sight to see Tinker coming along with a rabbit it had caught, legs straddled each side of the rabbit as it dragged it along.

One day when we got home from school, Mrs Westlake told us that Tinker had not been home all day and that she wondered what had happened. I took a sack and went around the hedges looking for it, calling out its name. After a while I found him, he was caught in a steel gin-trap by his paw. I released the paw but Tinker was struggling like anything so I put him in the sack and took him home. When I got there we couldn't touch him, he was spitting and howling at us, so we put him in the shed for the night. Next morning when I went to have a look at Tinker, there he was looking very sorry for himself and licking the paw. When we put food and milk down for him, he stopped licking and went for that instead. We thought it would stop Tinker going after rabbits but we were wrong, he carried on as usual.

THE POST LADY

The post lady used to ride from Higher Clovelly Post Office (at Turn Pike) and deliver to the houses and farms that were away from the village as well as those in Higher Clovelly. Her name was Mary and she would ride her bike in all weathers, delivering the mail, which was very welcome to me with a letter from my sister Violet and sometimes a letter from dad with the usual sixpenny or shilling postal order or maybe a parcel of comics.

MR & MRS WESTLAKE OF SOUTHDOWN COTTAGE

They gave me a home in Clovelly and Mr Westlake was a farm worker, what was called a good all-round man. He used to leave for work at about seven and normally did not get back home again until six o'clock in the evening, unless it was harvest time, then everyone on the farms works until it was dark. He worked at Burford Farm which was about two miles away and when he left home in the morning he would have his food in a satchel carried over his shoulder and a white billy-can on the handlebars.

When we children got home from school we would wait until he got home and by then we had washed our hands and sat waiting. It was agony sitting there, with the lovely smell of baking and cooking that came out of the oven, Then we would hear his bike coming through the front gate and he would come in. The white billy can would be filled with milk and sometimes he would have some rabbits for dinner next day. He would ask us how we got on at school and then off would come his heavy boots which he left outside in the porch, then he would wash and he would say the words we had been waiting for, "Bring your chairs to the table."

Oh those meals, plates loaded with food, seconds if you wanted it and I always did. After dinner he would roll himself a cigarette and if it was Spring or Summer, he would say that he was just going out into the garden to do some work for a while; or perhaps Mrs Westlake would tell him that we boys needed a haircut. Then I would have to take a chair out into the garden where he would use clippers and scissors on us. We used to wait for Mrs Westlake's words, "That's better father."

Mr Westlake was in the Home Guard and sometimes he had to go on duty. I can see him and Mr Slee now, riding off on their bikes, both dressed in their khaki uniforms with their rifles slung over their shoulders. Sometimes they had to go on duty to Hartland Point or Hartland Quay. I used to enjoy cleaning the rifle and polishing his boots for him as it seemed I was part of the Home Guard as well.

HARVEST TIME AND 'TEDDY' PICKING

The farmer who Mr Westlake worked for, allowed him a piece of a field in which to plant several rows of potatoes and each year he would take the seed potatoes that he had sprouted out at home and we would help him to plant them. Throughout the year, he would hoe and weed the rows in his spare time and when it came to harvesting them, we would go over to help him. Normally it would be Mr Westlake and myself digging them, picking the potatoes and collecting them in baskets and old buckets and then, when they were full, putting the potatoes into sacks. We would leave the sacks in rows across the field and after all the potatoes had been dug, Mr Westlake would borrow the horse and cart from the Farmer at Burford Farm and bring the load home.

Outside the cottage there was a shed called 'The Teddy House' and it was here that all the potatoes were emptied into a large boarded-off compartment. They used to last us right through the year, as well as provide food for the rats who loved them.

Although it was a back breaking job, I, like many other children, went potato (teddy) picking for different farmers. We were paid the standard rate of fourpence an hour and were allowed time off from school to do it.

CORN HARVEST

I would go and work for Mr Slee at corn harvest time, stacking and turning before the time came to carry. The binder would cut and tie the corn into sheaves and they would be lying all over the place. We would stack them up into sixes, two pairs sloping against each other and one at each end. They would then ripen off a bit more and a day or so later they could be carried.

The carrying was done with horse and carts and the loads would be built properly and I used to help Brian Slee on the loads and they could get quite high. Back and forward the horses would go with the loads to the farm yard to be built into stacks or ricks. If need be, to finish the field, we would work right into darkness and by the end we would be very tired and hungry. I used to get paid the usual fourpence an hour for this and one year I was paid twentyone shillings and sixpence for the harvest work – sixtyfour and a half hours.

When thrashing time came the machine would be placed beside the rick and the noise and dirt would be terrific. We children would gather around the rick, which usually had wire-netting surrounding it, and kill the rats as they came out. We were paid a penny a tail by the government for every rat that we killed, as the rats were eating and destroying a lot of food all over the country.

BATH NIGHT

Every Saturday evening was bath-night in those days. I would get the tin bath off the nail in the scullery wall, carry it into the living room and place it in front of the range. The water would have been heating up in kettles on the range and more cold water would be pumped to go in the bath. The two younger ones went in first and then I would carry the bath outside, empty it, refill it and then have my bath in the scullery, because I was older. The soap was carbolic and we used to smell so clean when we were sitting there in our clean pyjamas with our bed-time drink.

WINTER TIME

Walking to school in the winter time was an ordeal for we had to go such a long way and if it was snow, sleet or rain, it was usually accompanied by fierce winds and we would be very cold and wet by the time we got to school. We were glad when we got there and we used to stand around those lovely tortoise stoves to dry out and get warm. When we got home in the evening it would be starting to get dark. The door would be shut, the paraffin oil lamp lit and put on the table and its light and the glow from the fire, it was nice and snug. Mr Westlake would come in, we would all have

111

our meal and then out would come his baccy tin and he'd roll himself a cigarette. Sometimes we would have the wireless on and this was run on accumulators which I used to collect after they had been charged, from either the garage or Electricity House at Clovelly Cross.

MRS WESTLAKE'S NIGHT OUT

One night each week Mrs Westlake would go to a Whist Drive at Clovelly School. When it got dark in the winter nights, I went with her as an escort as far as Turn Pike and then I would stay with Granny Westlake, whilst Mrs Westlake went on to the school with other people. Afterwards, we would walk through the lanes with our arms linked, sometimes pitch dark, but as we knew the way, it was no problem; down Providence Hill, home, a hot drink and into bed.

MY SISTER'S VISIT

It was a hot summer day when I had a letter to say that my eldest sister was coming to see me. Violet had taken over the running of the home after mother had died and the thought of her coming down to see me got me very excited. She would be arriving at Southdown Cottage at a certain time and I remember running all the way back from school to meet her. As I arrived she was outside the cottage to meet me and we hugged and kissed until I saw a young man was there as well. She told me that they were engaged but that she had something special to tell me. They had just got married and were on their honeymoon and staying at Cleverton's Hotel in Bideford.

She was relieved that I was not upset about her getting married, seeing as how I had lost my mother a short while before and now was losing my big sister who was our acting mother. She told me that they had booked a room for me in the hotel for the following night. After we had our meal we all played cricket in the field by the side of the cottage until it began to get dark and then Bob and myself were taken into our neighbour's, Mrs Prowse, to sleep for the night, whilst my sister and her new husband had our bed.

The next day after breakfast, we caught the bus into Bideford, we sat by the river for some time then just strolled around, happy that we were together. She told me that dad had given her some money to buy me my first long trouser suit and we bought it from Hepworths in the High Street. The evening meal in the hotel was something that I shall always remember and then up to my room. I had never been in a hotel before and it was all so wonderful and strange.

Sadly I had to say goodbye to them the next day, when after a mid-day meal, I caught the two o'clock bus back to Clovelly. Sitting in the seat with the parcel containing my new suit on my lap, I waved to them until we were out of sight.

MY SATURDAY JOB

After a while and as I was older, Butcher Cruse asked me if I would like to help him and his daughter Joan deliver the meat around the area on a Saturday morning. I agreed and thereafter, every Saturday morning, after I had returned from Hartland at about eleven o'clock, we would set out in his little Ford van. It was the same van that had taken me to Southdown Cottage on the first occasion. Joan would drive, dressed in a brown overall coat and I would sit beside her. We would deliver meat to all the outlying farms and cottages, then to Higher Clovelly, Clovelly Court and then to the village.

The van would be left at the top of the cobbles and we would load as much meat as we could carry into big baskets. Then it was up and down the cobbles delivering meat to the people who lived in the little cottages perched on the side of the cliff. Back home again at about one o'clock, just in time for my meal, which usually was a pasty with brown sauce, a slice of yeast cake and a cup of tea.

NO SMOKING

In Higher Clovelly is a little group of houses and a farm that are called Burscott. When I was a boy, there was a gentleman living in a house there who was called Mr Godwin and he was well known in the area for the man who rode an old motor bike and who had a club foot. He was very well spoken and was not a local, although he had lived there for a number of years.

He took an interest in me and because he knew I loved singing and had a pretty good voice, he would invited me to his place to sing whilst he played the piano. One day he told me he had someone coming to tea and would I come along as well to sing. This was agreed and I met the people, Mr and Mrs Watson and we all sat down to have tea. Afterwards, Mr Godwin played the piano and then produced some music sheets and asked me to sing. I remember some of them – Drink to me only with thine eyes; Early one morning; Abide with me, and several others. It was a good evening and I returned home to Southdown.

Some weeks later, Mr Hesketh asked me if I would go into Bideford and sing in a show there in support of getting people to save for War Weapons Week. What had happened was that Mr and Mrs Watson's son Jack, who was in the Services, was to have appeared but he had been called back from leave.

To do the show, I had to have my father's permission and a telegram was sent to him that morning, for the show was in the evening. Someone went and got my clothes and tooth brush from Southdown and as the day went on, I still hadn't got my father's permission. The school day ended and we all started off for our homes but I had only got as far as Turn Pike when from the Post Office a boy came running waving a telegram. dad had given his permission for me to do the concert. Mr Hesketh gave some money for my fare on the bus and off I went to Bideford.

At Bideford, Mr Godwin was waiting for me and straight away he took me to Tanton's Hotel where we had a big slap-up tea. At about six o'clock a car came for us and took as to where the concert was to be held. I was to sing after the interval and meanwhile I was allowed to sit in the front and watch the other acts. Then into the artists dressing room and looking in the big mirrors in wonder at it all. Soon it my turn and up to the wings and when it was time, out onto the stage and when the curtains

113

went back, I sang. It was a selection from what I had sung in Mr Godwin's house in front of Mr and Mrs Watson.

After the show, I was driven back to Tanton's Hotel where a room had been booked for me and there on the bedside table was a plate of sandwiches and a stone jar of ginger beer. I was told to put my shoes outside the door of my room and they would be cleaned for me by morning, this was all so strange to me.

Breakfast next morning was something new for me. I was alone at the table when the waiter came and handed me the menu and asked what I would like for breakfast. I think I had nearly everything. Then it was time for the bus back to Clovelly, where I arrived back at about dinner time. I returned to school for the afternoon lessons and then at the end of the day I was glad to get to bed, after such an exciting time.

A few days later, Mr Hesketh gave me a Savings Certificate for fifteen shillings as payment for my part in the show and he told me that Mr Watson was a well known stage actor and performer who gave monologues and that his stage name was Nosmo King. I found out later that he said he had got the name from the No Smoking sign in a railway carriage. His son Jack, whose place I took, went on after the war, to become a famous stage and film actor. I often see him on TV. and think of the day I took his place.

COMING OF AGE

December 1942 came, I was fourteen years of age and it was time for me to return home to Bristol. I had Christmas at Southdown but in the New Year I had to say my goodbyes. Mr Hesketh gave me my train ticket to Bristol Templemeads and wished me well. I said goodbye to all my mates and school friends and started the walk back to Southdown from school, a walk I had done many times but would not be doing any more. I looked back at the school and thought of that first time that I had seen it, it seemed a hundred years before instead of just two short years. I never thought that I would feel this way about a school, but I had had some very happy times there with good friends and now that I was leaving it, I was very sad.

When I got back to Southdown, I went out again and walked into Hartland to say goodbye to my friend Tom Prowse, the cobbler, then back to say goodbyes to all the neighbours that had been so kind to me. Mr and Mrs Westlake gave me a Bible and Mr and Mrs Slee gave me a book about Jesus. That night I lay awake for a long time, I was conscious of the fact that my life in the country was ending, at the same time as my schooldays were over.

The next morning I was up early and after breakfast, dad's old kitbag came out again and I packed. Mr Westlake said goodbye to me and told me that I always had a home there with them if ever I wanted, then off he went to work. I went up into the garden once more to look around at everything, then it was time to catch the bus. I picked the loaded kitbag and this time it was easier for me, I was bigger and stronger than when I had first come to live at Southdown.

Mrs Westlake and Mary walked with me to the bus stop, with Tinker the cat, following behind. The bus was coming. We kissed and we hugged and we cried.

Promises to write and then I was away. We waved to each other for some time until they were lost to sight.

I met my father at Bideford Railway Station. He had just come down on the train and we waited a while then boarded. We were on our way. I was leaving Devon. We changed trains at Taunton for Bristol Templemeads and the train appeared to be full of sailors who were going home on leave, they were happy and singing. When dad told them I had been evacuated and that he was just bringing me home again, they gave me bars of chocolate. By the time that we arrived in Bristol it was dark

Waiting for us at the station was my big brother in his sailor's uniform and we got a taxi home. I remember getting out of the taxi in our street and thinking how all the houses

Jeanie Goulding with her brother John.

seemed so small and the streets so narrow. The day had been a long one and after greeting everyone who was there to meet me, I had something to eat and then went to bed.

MEMORIES

Outside the Retreat, summer of 1941.

L to R
Jeanie Goulding,
Doris Dobson,
Pat Reid

My memories of Clovelly in those war time years are of a crowded school, with over two hundred children from London, Bristol and Plymouth as well as the locals. The playground full of shouting children running about and making such a noise that it was said they could hear it way down in the village.

Running down to the canteen at dinner times, having plenty to eat, second helpings of chocolate pudding and custard and then, full up, running (waddling) all the way back across the fields to school.

All of us boys with spades, hoes, rakes and forks over our shoulders, walking up the road to Wonnacott's, whistling as we went, we were digging for victory.

Playing in the field in front of Court House, I think it is called The Lawn. There we would play football, cricket and other games with Mr Hesketh always joining in and enjoying himself.

The boys who were my pals or school friends were:Harry Littley, from London, lived in the village; Dick Rockall and George Mitchell, from London, lived at Hugglepit Farm; Harry Clement, from London, lived at Crossland Farm; George Smith from Clovelly, lived at Higher Clovelly; Ray Lamb, from London, lived at Slerra, Clovelly; Fred Morgan and Ken Hicks, from Plymouth, lived at New Inn Hotel; Royston Hill and Tony Hill from Bristol, lived at Southdown Farm

CHAPTER TEN

A TODDLER'S TALES

My memories of those early years, around the beginning of 1939, at least sometime before the Second World War started, was, at the age of five, running errands, sometimes to get hot bread straight from the baker's ovens, or the butcher's, clasping a note of what was required, in case I forgot why I was running the errand. The few pence that these things cost could be trusted with me and with the carrier bag in one hand and the money in the other, I would set off. I can still hear my mother's voice ringing after me, 'Say please and thank you in the shop'.

If I was lucky, I would sometimes have some empty jam jars to return to the oil shop where I could get a penny for each clean unchipped jar. The money obtained would be spent on a variety of things from sweets, comics or toy soldiers.

My school was Bellenden Road School and it appeared to me to be miles away from my home and it was a shock, much later in my life, to discover that it was in fact only about 300 yards away. At school I always wanted to be an ink monitor or any other important job, just to impress my teacher, Miss Blackmore, with whom I was very much in love. I thought it strange that she never seemed to feel the same way about me, except maybe a pat on the head, or other end, depending on how I was behaving.

In those days before the war, every day was summer, or so it seemed and schooldays were highlighted by events such as St.George's Day when children in organisations such as the Scouts, Guides, Cubs, Brownies and Boy's Brigade attended school in their uniforms with flags etc. Those children who were not in uniform just looked on with envy.

All those summer days were dispelled in September 1939, when we were at war with Germany, and although it appeared exciting at first when we were issued with little brown cardboard boxes on a piece of string with a thing called a gas mask inside, the novelty soon wore off. Most of us did not like the smell of the gas mask and when we were ordered to wear them in class for gas drill, most of us felt as though we were choking and took them off again.

There came the day when my mum told my brother, sister and I that we would be going on a holiday away from London and that we would be going on a train. 'Won't that be exciting', she had said. It was, until a man pinned a label on my jacket and took me out of my mum's arms at Peckham Rye Railway station. I remember seeing on my mother's lapel, a Royal Navy badge and one for the RAF and now as an adult I can reflect what she must have been thinking, the torture she must have been going through – three teenage sons in the Forces, a daughter in the Women's Land Army and the three youngest off to heavens knew where, or to what.

I do not actually remember the train journey to Bideford, but on our arrival at Clovelly I was impressed with all the greenery instead of bricks and concrete and we were allocated to our new homes... How my sister gloated when she was told she was going to Dyke Green Farm with all the animals, and then the powers that be decided that it would be more suitable for two boys than a single girl. I am sure she never forgave them for that.

It was on this farm with Mr and Mrs Bill Johns that we spent the next two years of our lives. My adopted Grandad always wore knee length gaiters, and in his pocket he carried a pen-knife, the sole purpose of which appeared to be cutting off bits of turnip that he was in the habit of pulling in the garden. He was continuously offering pieces to us, saying, 'Go on taste a bit, it'll do you good'. Maybe that is why my wife always leaves this particular vegetable off from my plate when serving dinner.

Dyke Green Farm was where I first met Royston. He was one of the grandsons of Mr and Mrs Johns, and although he was only about five to six years older that me, he appeared huge and a lot older than I suppose he really was. He was a good friend to have around.

Grandad had two massive shire type horses, the grey named Prince and the black named Model, and they used to look beautiful in their harness with all the brasses gleaming. Sometimes, as a special treat, Royston would walk them alongside the granary steps where my brother and I would clamber up onto their broad backs for a ride.

On coming home from school one day, I heard a terrible squealing noise coming from the direction of the pig-pens. I, in all innocence, thinking that pigs, like all other animals were pets and never associating them with food that was put on the plate, ran towards the pig-pens and was confronted with such a terrible sight that shattered my faith in so many things and people. They were slaughtering the pigs and even my friend Royston was taking part in this horrible act.

The kitchen in the farm house was always warm and inviting, with the table alongside one wall, on which all meals were taken by, it seemed, everybody at anytime. There was another room leading off from the kitchen and in here we could sit and read. There was a further room which was absolutely out of bounds to children with grubby hands; we must always have been grubby as we were never allowed into that room.

Sunday was a special day when we were taken to chapel, when we would be given strict instructions that there was to be no whistling of any kind and that if we wanted to sing, then it must only be hymns.

Harvest Festival in the chapel was something not to be forgotten, a sight to see and it took your breath away. Flowers, fruit and vegetables were everywhere, all types, shades and sizes and it appeared that people only managed to sit in between the displays. Sadly the chapel is no a place of worship, some years ago it was converted into a private residence.

From the beauty of Clovelly, a haven of peace and tranquillity, I returned all too soon to London with my brother and sister. In London my playground of fields, farm buildings and woods were exchanged for bomb sites, my toys became pieces of shrapnel and spent bullet cases. This was a far cry from the beautiful countryside that I had grown to know and love, but I was home in the family fold and with the ending of the war, all my brothers and sisters returned home unscathed from their war-time experiences. Although my memories of Clovelly are happy ones, I cannot help, as I look at my grandson, reflect that I am glad he is who he is today, and not as I was, an evacuee.

CHAPTER ELEVEN
FROM COALYARD TO PROVIDENCE

The world of cat's meat shops -where you could buy a pennyworth of sliced horse meat on a wooden skewer for your pet, have long since gone; similarly disappeared are the days when you could have your hundredweight of 'Best kitchen nuts' coal delivered by the coalman, who drove a lovely horse pulling a flat-backed cart with a very high driving seat, or hear the calls of the greengrocer as he made his rounds of the streets, selling the best of produce from his small four-wheeled cart pulled by a smart little cob horse. Such was the village-like communities in prewar south London, especially Deptford, where I was born and first went to school.

Hitler changed all of that when he started to bomb and invade other countries and Britain was at war with Germany. My little world of friendly neighbours and little houses packed with people who cared for one another, was soon to come to a sudden and dramatic end. The grimey streets, close to the River Thames, were full of friendly people, who although were definitely not cockneys, had as many of the cockney's good points. Most of them were poor, even when they were in work, and most of their necessities were bought from the local shops on credit, although it was not called that. 'On the slate' or the 'Harry Tate' was the system of obtaining the food from the shop and the shop-keeper would write the amount down against the person's name in a little book. Settling up time came when the man of the house brought home his weekly wages, such as it was.

My parents, Violet and Tom Goulding, had a business at 17, Gosterwood Street, Deptford, and we lived above the shop. My dad had a horse and cart and he delivered coal to the houses around the area, keeping his horse in a stable at the back of the house and the cart and the coal was kept in the yard nearby. Dad also had a timber yard around the back of the house and he supplied local builders with their wood and in the shop, which my mum managed, they sold things that were connected with building. So we were fortunate in my family, dad having different things to fall back on if one part of his business slowed down, and anyway, in those days, a lot of people cooked on kitchen ranges fuelled by coal.

Even though I was only four when war was declared and not really knowing what it was all about, some of the conversation between my parents or them and our neighbours, reached out to me and the impression I have is that I knew something was happening, perhaps terrible, as it was upsetting adults, but to me it meant very little. How all that was to change.

Exciting things were happening around Deptford, with trenches and air-raid shelters being dug in Deptford Park and up on Greenwich Common, huge shiny silver balloons floating in the air above our houses and along the Thames and I remember

Wedding of Joan Cruse and Johnny Searles in 1942
Bridesmaids: Jeanie Goulding, Jill Gadd, Pat Reid

the inquisitiveness as a small child of asking why the men were diggingup the grass and making deep holes where we used to play or have picnics. Some of the trenches and shelters had fences around them to stop the local children exploring.Then came gas mask fitting down at the church hall. Along we went as a familyand I remember my aunt and uncle being there with my cousin who was much younger than me, and the fuss there was when my cousin was given a Mickey Mouse type mask and my brother John and I had to have the same kind as the adults.

I remember going to school one day with my brother and this was to be the day when a lot of the children in my school were to be evacuated. I was carrying my gasmask in the cardboard box with the string around my shoulders; in my pocket I had sticks of barley sugar to eat during the journey. My mum was walking beside us, carrying my case. I was wearing a white coat, black shoes, blue crepe dress with white trim. I had a label tied through my lapel, on which was written my name and address. My mum must have been worried about me getting lost, as she had put small labels on all of my clothes so it didn't matter what I was wearing, my name and address was on that item of clothing.

From the school I remember going on a bus and arriving at a railway station and then getting on a train. I don't really recall what I thought at the time, I suppose I thought no more of it than having a day out. The train journey was long but I don't remember too much about it except that at one point we were given cakes to eat and that Pat Reid dropped some crumbs onto the floor. One of the teachers that came with us from our school, happened to see them and shouted to Pat to clear them up. I knew Pat, she lived next door to me in Deptford and I knew a lot of the other children as well, because our few streets back home in those days were like a little village where everyone knew everyone and you all helped one another. On the train was Doris Dobbins from our street as well as George Mitchell and Ken Thomas and Colin Williams, who came from a couple of streets away.

On arrival in Bideford we had a wash and something to eat, then some of us were taken in motor cars to a hostel at Parkham. Either we were not required to stay or they had no room for us because we were soon on our way to Clovelly by bus.

When we got to our destination we found that the other children we had left in Bideford had just arrived as well and we all stood in lines on the grass outside the big house. People came around, looking at us, reading our labels and then talking among themselves. I remember a girl, who I later knew to be Hilda Braund, saying to her mother that she wanted to choose me, but at that moment, Doris Dobbins, who was about four years older than me and who had been told by my mum to look after me, said very loudly that I couldn't go without her as we had to go together.

Doris and I stayed together and a lady came up and chose both of us and Pat Reid and led us away. This was my first meeting with anyone from the Cruse family and this lady was one of the daughters, Barbara, who we children learnt to address as Auntie Barbara. Off we walked from Court House to the village.

Now Clovelly village is outstanding in that it is unique for having a narrow cobbled High Street down the side of the cliffs and where motor traffic is banned. It is beautiful, a village of pretty flower covered cottages overlooked by magnificent woods and with a small harbour at the bottom. As we walked down the steep High Street I noticed a lady standing in the middle of the street some way down. She was dressed just like a fairy godmother and I thought she was so beautiful with her long blonde hair and this lovely dress. As we got nearer she greeted Barbara and we three girls. This was Barbara's sister Mary, with whom she shared a cottage known as Providence House which was in the High Street. It transpired that Mary had been chosen as the Carnival Queen and was wearing the dress for the carnival that day. I still remember it was mauve with white sleeves.

We girls were shown up to our bedroom in a little attic room, right at the top and where we were to spend many happy hours. To get to it you had to climb a very narrow staircase and I recall the room had a sloping ceiling on which, even as children, we were always banging our heads.

When the time came for me to attend school, I was taken to a little chapel in the village which had been turned into a schoolroom for the younger children, whilst the older ones went to the village school at Wrinkleberry. As Auntie Barbara was the village school's infants teacher, she taught us.

I remember that the days seemed to be crowded with things to do, things to learn and see; places to explore around the village as well as further afield in the woods and the cliff tops. There seemed to be a lot of people living in the village at that time, many of them not local and one family who I got to know very well were the Bonham-Carters, who I believe were friends or relatives of the lady of the manor, Mrs Betty Asquith. I remember Lady Bonham-Carter was very kind to me and often had me in their cottage, she had others of her family with her and one was her son Mark who would have been in his late teens then. Lady Bonham-Carter gave me a lovely game which consisted of pieces of card, blank on one side and a part of a fish on the other. The cards were dealt face down and you had to see who could build the fish and get rid of the cards in your hand the fastest. I still have that game to this very day. Being only five years old, I used to enjoy Mark giving me 'piggy-backs' up North Hill, a very steep alternative way to the top of the village; if we could meet now I somehow don't think he would repeat the journey. Those were very happy days for me.

Being a city girl I loved the open spaces, the countryside and nature. Picking and learning all the different kinds of flowers, watching newts in the farm ponds and trying to remember all the names of the various birds that we saw.

Mrs Asquith opened her home to lots of evacuees and I seem to remember there were young girls who were not part of our evacuee group and some of them spoke English with a slight foreign accent. I believe they were children of foreign friends of Mrs Asquith. Often we would have parties and games in one of the rooms called Long Passage, which was a long low ceilinged room with, I remember, a tiled floor, black and white I believe. The parties always meant we had musical chairs, which we loved and usually produced a lot of noise and laughter. Shows would be put on for us by adults and older children, then later we started getting involved ourselves. I remember one lad from Deptford named Ken, used to do impersonations of Hitler, ridiculing him in a way that had us screaming with delight at his antics. He had his hair brushed the wrong way across his forehead and wore a false moustache. This boy was billeted with the Cruse family at their home at 'The Retreat'; Uncle Jim Cruse, the father of Barbara and Mary was the local butcher and already had several boys living in the rooms above the shop.

One way we could repay Mrs Asquith for her kindness was to help her whenever we could and one such way was where she wanted the yellow ragwort plants pulled up in the field just in front of Court House. This was The Lawn in which we held our school sports and games, and when we children were not using it, her horses and ponies grazed there. I understood that the ragwort was regarded as a poisonous plant to some animals and so was usually pulled up. I remember the stalks were tough and for a little girl it made it harder. I know they used to hurt my hands and at first I became alarmed when I saw the stain on my fingers but as time went on, I got used to these country ways.

I loved the walks through Mrs Asquith's park, along the cliff tops to Gallantry Bower and those through West Woods down to the beach at Mouth Mill. Those exploring walks through the Hobby Drive where in the Spring, I could see the bluebells and the bunches of London Pride by the first bridge, are still in my memory and I still enjoy my walks through the Hobby.

Other things that have stayed in my mind are the swimming lessons in the harbour, that the teachers gave to us children whilst the fishermen and their families looked on in amusement. The radio personality – Nosmo King, who was a great favourite with us children and whenever he was on the beach he was sure to have a group of children around him and his wife as he told us stories or made up little poems. I remember once a lady and a gentleman sitting on the quay and someone said they were Anne Zeigler and Webster Booth. To prove the point, one of the children went and asked them if they were the famous singing duo and once we had confirmation our news quickly spread throughout the village.

As time went on I left the old chapel classroom in the village and went up to the village school named Wrinkleberry. It is in a beautiful setting and I doubt whether any other school has such lovely views from the playground. In the early 1940's the school was a very crowded place with more than two hundred evacuees from London, Bristol and Plymouth being added to the forty or so local children.

I can still remember the green curtains that were hung across the room, or was it the hall, to separate it into classrooms; I think they made three or four divisions and with the two smaller classrooms leading off from the big room, it gave some five or six classes. I recall vividly the pandemonium during class work of the noise coming from behind the curtain where other children were having a different lesson, equally I remember the huge pot bellied stoves that heated the school, two in the big room, one each in the other two. They burnt coke and always had a bowl of water on top to absorb the fumes and on the metal guards that surrounded them, often hung the wet coats of those who had walked two or three miles to school. In the wintertime, these children would place their pasties or other food, on the stove to warm up prior to the mid-day break.

The local headmaster was Mr Hesketh, assisted by Auntie Barbara, Mr Bamsey and Miss Plaice from Peckham and Miss Woods from Deptford, although she didn't stay long, and Miss Williams from Plymouth. Mr Hesketh ruled the school with very strict discipline and would cane boy and girl alike if he felt that they deserved it.

He caned me once in front of the school because he was trying to get at my brother John. Mr Hesketh had John out in front of his class and was telling him off for being lazy over his reading and said, "… even your little sister reads better than you". He then called me out from my class (behind another curtain) and told me to read what John was having trouble with, I suppose to make an example of John and make him look silly in front of his mates. However I wasn't having any of it and refused to read the passage, this got Mr Hesketh mad and he caned me on both hands. He certainly was not my favourite teacher after that.

Mr Hesketh was supported in the caning policy by most of the other teachers, after all it was generally accepted throughout all the schools in the country at that time. I remember Miss Williams caning one boy for something and this particular boy (a local boy) suffered very badly from chilblains on his hands. Nevertheless she intended to cane him and as the first stroke came down he moved his hand away and she following through with the stroke hit her own leg a powerful whack. This made her very angry and she proceeded her hit him again and again. Of course his bleeding chilblains were bleeding worse than ever and there was a lot of murmuring among the children. There was a great fuss next day when the boy's father came up to school and threatened retribution for what had been done to his son. The result of all this was the boy was transferred to the next village at Hartland.

I remember once, Miss Williams had probably had enough of us that particular day and said that the next child who made a noise would be caned. Stupidly I said, "Ooh", very softly and thinking she wouldn't hear. But I was wrong, she heard and said, "Who made that noise"? Straight away a girl, Violet Ray from Plymouth, said, "Jeanie Goulding miss ". Of course Miss Williams shouted, "Come out here, hold out your hand". Thinking I could avoid punishment I said, "My mum said to tell you that if you caned me once more she'll come up to school after you the next time she comes down to see me". Well I got an extra two for my cheek, but my mum did go to see her and tell her a few home truths when she came down to see me.

Group of evacuees from Peckham and Deptford at Bucks Mills beach. Summer 1940
Miss Plaice (teacher) in atterndance

Playtimes in the schoolyard was like Piccadilly Circus in the rush hour, with children rushing about or collected together into friendly groups. Boys were separated from the girls by a five foot high stone wall, and after the little chapel in the village ceased to be used as a classroom, Wrinkleberry accommodated all children from 5 years to 14 years. There were no toilets within the school building, they were reached across the yard and water for washing your hands was obtained from a pump on the outside of the toilet wall. During the winter this pump was invariably frozen solid but even if it wasn't, the freezing cold water did not enhance its use for hygiene purposes.

Sometimes various groups or committees like the Red Cross, Spitfire Fund, Navy Fund etc.,would organise a whist drive and social at the school. They would be held in the big room with the curtains being unhooked and the chairs being placed around the walls. It was always the whist drive first, then a break for tea and cakes and then we would have the social. The socials were mixed age affairs and would generally consist of games, ordinary dancing and folk-dancing to a four or five piece band and most of the children were allowed to attend them as they usually finished before ten thirty and were normally held on a Saturday evening. I can recall how dark it was when we left the school and walked home along the lanes; there were no lights being shown out at sea or around the bay like there are today.

Although it was a very long time ago, I can remember as if it were yesterday the time my father came down to see me and meeting him as he got off the bus. I was so proud of him in uniform and I knew that my dad, like so many others, was fighting in the war and if was alright, then we were going to beat the Germans.

As England was at war even we children had to do our bit to help. Boys were digging for victory in that they were growing food for the school canteen, girls were sometimes employed in the kitchen to prepare and cook the food with proper adult staff supervising us. The older girls would go out with the boys collecting metal and paper for salvage and they would travel miles with either wheelbarrows, old prams, or in the winter, sledges, which they would pull through the snow, loaded with as much scrap metal as they could manage. Another thing that the girls were organised into groups to help the war effort, was knitting things for the troops, although I suppose some went to the navy and airforce as well. I often wonder what the boys looked like when they wore the results of our knitting, but if they were cold, I don't suppose they mattered much.

Harvest time meant that school attendance was slack and the authorities did not bother to ask too many questions if they knew you had been helping with the harvest instead of being at school. This mainly applied to the older children, but we soon found that there were jobs for even the younger ones, perhaps taking the tea in baskets out to the men in the fields, or collecting the empty cups when they had finished. harvest time was also an excuse to stay up late and I can still remember the wonderful feeling of being in the fields long after I should have been in bed. As there was 'double summer time' during the war it was often quite light up to eleven o'clock in the summer.

Sometimes I went down to Home Farm to see if I could help and the farmer's wife, Mrs Peggy Burrows, would let me help her preparing huge meals for the workers when they had finished for the day. I remember the Italian prisoners-of-war that were working on the land, they used to wear brown battledress uniforms with yellow 'POW' on them and later in the war, they used to walk or rides bikes around the lanes and were quite friendly. The Italians used to tell us that they never wanted to fight in the war and they sometimes gave us gifts, like baskets that they had made. I wonder how many girls have still got these little presents. They were replaced by German prisoners-of-war but they were a sullen lot and didn't want to talk to any of us and none of us liked them.

By now, I was living at The Retreat, the home of Auntie Mary's parents. That was on the main Clovelly to Hartland road and was about two miles from the school. Auntie Mary had gone into the army (A.T.S.) and Auntie Barbara moved back home and took us children with her. At The Retreat we found that there were also other evacuees and we soon settled down with them all. Every morning when we set out for school, we soon became a sizeable group as we met up with other local and evacuee children as we passed each cottage and farm and then Auntie Barbara would cycle past us and tell us to get a move on or we would be late for school.

Auntie Joan, who helped her father with the butchers business, had met a soldier who was stationed on a gun or searchlight site at Clovelly and they became engaged. Everything was so exciting when the wedding was being arranged and three of us girl evacuees were asked to be bridesmaids to Auntie Joan; there was Jill Gadd, Pat Reid and myself, and of course we were thrilled to bits, especially when we had to go into the next village at Hartland to be fitted for our dresses. I suppose we really thought that we were something special and couldn't wait to tell all the other girls at school.

I suppose another major occurrence of those times was when the British Wellington bomber crashed in Higher Clovelly, in fact across the lane along which we walked to school and near to West Dyke Farm and Hugglepit Cross. When we got to where the plane had crashed, we saw that the remains of it was in the fields either side of the lane and had ploughed through the hedges. There were lots of soldiers and airmen working there with lorries and things and they lifted us children over the mud and debris in the lane. I heard afterwards that all the crew had been killed.

There was the time when my brother told me that he had heard from home that our house had been bombed. A doodle-bug had hit the house but our mum and dad and grandfather were alright. Some friends of my parents had been away from their house when it got hit the same day and someone in the next street, Folkestone Gardens, had given them somewhere to stay. The next day that house was hit and they were all killed.

It was obvious to even we young children that the war couldn't last much longer and there came the time when my brother told me that he was being taken back to London. Now I was a shy girl, a bit of a loner really and I became afraid once I knew my brother was leaving me, even though we did not live in the same house in Clovelly.

My mum came down to collect Johnny and I told her her my fears and she reluctantly agreed to take me as well. The preparation for my return was therefore very hurried, overnight in fact. Mum was staying elsewhere in Clovelly and it was arranged that she and Johnny would come up with Mr Squires, the carrier, and that I would meet them at Clovelly Cross the next morning.

The parting was lots of tears on the part of the Cruse's and myself. The raids were still on in London, in that the flying bombs were still killing people in the capital and I was going from the safety of a good home to the uncertainty of wartime London.

The day of my leaving was 25th May 1945 and Auntie Barbara took me to Clovelly Cross to meet Mr Stan Squires. As his lorry pulled up I saw that my mum and Johnny were in the back. Auntie Barbara was crying, I was crying, but I had to go now I had got this far. I remember even the clothes that I wore that day – a check coat with a velvet collar, and a black velour hat. Mr Squires took us to Bideford station where we caught the train to London. Here I saw red buses that I hadn't seen for ages.

This was not the London that I had left five years earlier, with bomb damage all around. There was not much left of our street and I saw the ruins of our old house, the house in which I had been born. Now it was only a pile of bricks and rubble, like so many of its neighbours. It was good to see my grandparents and aunties again and Mum had got accommodation for us in a nearby street, 83, Glosterwood, and it was there that I started to settled down in my new environment.

The end of the war with Germany came and was celebrated by everyone with street parties. Trestle tables covered in bed sheets and laid out with food that people had been saving their ration coupons for. Even in food rationing, everyone managed to put on a good spread, mainly for us children.

I know that war is a terrible thing and that so many innocent people got killed in the 1939-1945 war, but to many of us children, those that were welcomed with love by perfect strangers, we were the lucky ones, even if we did have our moments of heartache and yearning for our families and home.

The fact that I had left the Cruse family in 1945 did not mean I lost touch with them. On the contrary, I wrote to them often and took my school holidays from London to be with them. I visited them regularly throughout my life until I have now come to live in Clovelly once again, this time with my own family.

CHAPTER TWELVE

THE UNHAPPY CHILD

In 1939 I was attending Peckham Rye School in Whorlton Road, Peckham in South London but in October 1939, after war had been declared, I started at Bellenden Road School, Peckham.

Life in Peckham had changed quite a bit during the twelve months prior to the war starting; air-raid   shelters were being dug in the parks and commons – Peckham Rye looked like a building site, and 'Shelter' signs were going up everywhere, even outside ordinary shops that were offering the dubious safety of their cellars, via the entrance flaps on the pavement. Being the eldest in the family, I took my younger brothers and sisters to have their gas masks fitted in the hall in Queen Street, Peckham, and that was a palaver in itself. It appeared that none of the children liked the smell of the rubber of the mask and when they were fitted, they, like all of us, felt as though they were being gagged and wanted to rip them off.

Barrage balloons were flying over most of London and it seemed every open bit of space had a lorry and a winch with a cable holding the giant balloons in place. These were generally manned by the RAF and they would let us children close to their lorries to see how the winch worked. I remember the winch was in a sort of metal cage and they told us that was for protection in case the cable snapped on the winch. Occasionally you could see a balloon sailing across London with its cable and ropes dangling from it and we knew then that it had broken free from the lorry; there used to be rumours that the RAF shot them down but I don't really know how they retrieved them.

During the 'Munich Crisis' my brother and I had been evacuated with the school to Petworth in Sussex and we were there when war was declared in the September. We were billeted in a fine servant-run house but saw very little of the owners, and this meant that we had a pretty lonely sort of life. We were not allowed to mix with the owners during meal times or evenings, so we spent a lot of time in the kitchen with the maids. Our mother came to collect us in October 1939 and we returned to our home in Chadwick Road, Peckham.

Our attendance at Bellenden Road School, was like all the other children at this time, only part-time. I don't really know whether this was because there was a shortage of teachers through 'call-up' or that they had been evacuated. It became obvious that all those children whose parents wished to be evacuated would be going off to the country somewhere and I know that I did not view this prospect with any enthusiasm, having sampled one spell with a reluctant host in Petworth.

When the time came for us to be evacuated, it was in June 1940, and I think the authorities considered it unsafe for us to remain any longer as the war in France was going badly. I don't remember much about the journey, I might have closed my mind to it all and just held onto my brother, facing the inevitable. I do recall arriving in Clovelly and in spite of my loud protests that my brother and I were not to be split up, we were taken away from each other, I being paired with another girl whose brother had been taken away from her, and the two boys were put together. I suppose even then, it would not have been so bad if we were to be living close to each other, but the authorities deemed otherwise, and whilst my brother and the other boy were billeted down in the cobbled village of Clovelly, the other girl and I were taken to distant part of Higher Clovelly, which meant that the boys would only see their older sisters about once a week.

This unhappy state of affairs did not auger well for a pleasant stay; we were already very unhappy to be taken away from our parents and home surroundings and now to be split up from each other and put into strange homes really brought the curtains of unhappiness down with a bang. At times I felt that matters could not be worse if the Germans had come: if they did, I would have preferred to be with my mother than these strange people from whom I could not detect any degree of warmth or loving kindness.

When I think back to those times, I still consider that those responsible performed a terrible act in separating a little five year old boy from his older sister; the only person in his family that remained for him to cling to. The effect must have been traumatic and he was in fact, very distressed, and this had an immediate re-action on his behaviour in his billet, where the people were all very old and certainly not used to dealing with a broken hearted little boy.

At first I could not go to see him as I did not know where he was staying, and if I did, I did not know how to get there. After a day or so, I did manage to get to see him and I know that the other girl was similarly unhappy about being separated.

Eventually, the the mother of the other boy and girl came down to Clovelly and rented a cottage and took them with her and my brother came up to stay with me. That was much better for us both, although we felt that we were very unwelcome. Talking to lots of other evacuees made me realise that we were very unfortunate and that most of the children were very happy in their new homes.

I have tried to analyse the position many times since and I don't think it was always the fault of my brother or myself. An example would be when we were walking to school – just over a mile – and would sometimes be passed by a car containing our foster father and his children. As far as we were concerned, that was pure luxury in those days, but we were not to share it. I can understand now, some of the difficulties they must have felt with me – a thirteen year old and well developed. It must have been a heavy responsibility for them.

The first winter (1940) was very bad, and with snow and ice everywhere it was a job getting to school at Wrinkleberry, which is the name of the village school. I liked school but Mr Hesketh, the Headmaster, was something else, he ruled the school with a rod of iron, or rather, a cane, which he would use on boy and girl alike and he certainly didn't pat you with it. I well recall the dentist visiting the school with a nurse. They would use one of the three classrooms and we children would be called in one by one. If an extraction was required, it would be done there and then, no gas, no anaesthetic, just the nurse holding your head in a vice like grip whilst the dentist yanked the tooth out. That happened to me, and after the tooth was taken out I was told to return to my class and the next child's name was called.

Thinking back to those school days, I can recall Mr Bamsey and Miss Plaice from Peckham and another young lady teacher, I think from Plymouth. We girls thought that Miss Plaice was rather mod and with it, she tried to teach us girls deportment and to be 'young ladies'. Another 'nice' thing from those days was the plain dark chocolate that we could buy from the shop, on ration of course, and government controlled. It was more bitter than the chocolate of today and not so sweet, but it was a welcome extra to most of us children. You could say it was part of the sensible war-time diet that was so healthy for many of us

Because of our foster parent's attitude, I was not allowed out very much, and then not to go very far from the house. Luckily there was a farm not so very far away, and they welcomed me with open arms. They were so kind and friendly and taught me so much about the country. The farmer taught me to milk a cow, which was something for a London girl to achieve, and I was very proud when I filled my first pail of milk. There was also a cottage nearby where a widow lived who was a lovely lady and always made me very welcome. There was no chance that we could change billets because both the farmer and the widow lady had their share of evacuees already.

On the main Bideford road is a house called London Lodge, and there used to be two elderly ladies living there. They liked me and were very kind to me at the time; sadly I cannot remember their names but one was a relative of the Cadbury family and we always saw them together as they walked along the roads and lanes. I was welcome at their home, which was at one of the entrances to the Hobby Drive, a lovely private roadway under the spreading branches of the trees. The Hobby Drive was off from the main Bideford road and wound its way along the cliff-tops until it reached Clovelly village. Here was heaven for anyone, especially those of us from London, at various times of the year you could pick flowers, nuts or leaves; it was always a haven.

On these walks, mostly accompanied by either or both of the two ladies, they would show and name the various trees and flowers for us. I remember they showed us how to put tiny beads into the centre of small sea-shells and then paint them and make brooches from them.

As I grew older, one of the ladies said that she would like me to become a children's nurse and live-in with one of the Cadbury family. I suppose I was too young to grasp the significance of this kind offer.

After a while, my brother and I were allowed to walk down to Clovelly village and when we did, we normally chose to go by way of the Hobby Drive, and as we were not allowed to stay away too long, it meant that we couldn't dawdle in the Drive to admire nature. In the summer time I would dive off the top quay in the harbour and I loved swimming, at least until the fishermen put two sharks on the beach, that they said had been tearing their nets. After that, every shadow I saw on the water was a shark as far as I was concerned.

I believe the underlying unhappiness of our separation must have somehow been conveyed in my letters to my mother in London and as she was working hard to keep us all, could not come down to see us. She remained working in London right through the blitz and eventually she sent for us to return home to Peckham.

So after just fifteen months of evacuation we returned to blitzed old London. I remember there were many evacuees returning home and the newspaper reporters were there to greet the train at Waterloo Station, as well as parents. I have a newspaper cutting with a terrific photograph of my mum greeting my brother (I'm not in the photo). The reporter writes, 'Folly of the Switchback – Two thousand mothers and children left London for the reception areas the week before last and according to official estimate, a much larger number returned'. They reported my mother as saying," We haven't seen each other for 15 months. I couldn't afford to visit them because all my extra money went on their clothes. We just had to see each other, and this seemed the cheapest way. I will send him back if the raids start again. Maybe I could go away with them both".

Before I had left Clovelly, they had put a horrible black hat on my head, but before we actually caught the bus, I sneaked out and picked some field mushrooms for my mum and filled the hat with them. The pity was that by the time I got home they were all maggoty and we were unable to eat them. As my mum said, it was a lovely thought.

As our stay in our billet had not been a happy one, we did not keep in touch, although I did come down as a teenager and enquired after them but did not see them, and similarly I returned in about 1976 with my husband but again did not see them. Many years had elapsed since those war-time days and as I have said, our billet was not a happy home for us, although I am often reminded fondly of the farmer and the widow in the cottage – they were very kind to me.

Thinking back, perhaps the reason for all the unhappiness was that the foster parents were too young to have more children thrust upon them and could not cope. He was a hard man, leastways with us.

Still trying to reason it all out, I realise that one is not very understanding at twelve or thirteen years of age, but I feel saddened now when I think back and imagine my grandson at that age being taken from home, – yes I feel sad that perhaps I didn't understand more – maybe I did -it's a long time ago. All I know is how easy it was to forget them all.

THE RE-UNION

ROSE

I will try to express my feelings about going back to Clovelly for the re-union in 1990.

This was fifty years after the evacuees had arrived for the first time and here we were many of us meeting again for the first time since we had said our goodbyes in the 1940's.

It was lovely meeting old friends again and going to places we had almost forgotten and for me, my husband John and my brother George it was a terrific experience.

My thoughts are all tumbling out haphazard, seeing the school and the fact that it had changed little over the years, evacuees who I would not have remembered except that we all had name cards on our lapels and then renewing friendships with local people, who had been invited to the re-union. Of course, John and I had invited my old friends Norrie and Rachael with their husbands.

Going to church again was very moving for me and it was good to see that it was full and standing room only at the back. The bells were ringing, the church looked lovely and there was a happy atmosphere about the place. In the church, I met more friends and saw more local people; Joan Searles, who I first knew as Joan Cruse was sitting behind me with her husband Johnny, who had been a soldier at Clovelly when she married him in the war. I remembered Joan and her dad, the butcher, when they used to bring the meat down through the village.

The Thanksgiving Service certainly was lovely and there was nothing left unsaid by the Rev.Derek Bates. The service brought back so many happy memories.

The Hon.Mrs Mary Rous spoke to me and I reminded her that we had met before and that I had been to Clovelly Court many times to help the Red Cross in the war, to give blood and was also invited to her wedding.

My thoughts on the gathering in the Parish Hall, the food, speeches and drinks, was that it was all so very very happy. Even the background music was correct, as it was recordings of war-time music and songs, including our Vera Lynn. There were so many photographs being taken, it seemed by everyone, friends to meet and talk to, addresses to exchange and then more food and drinks. Then came the dancing. It was no good saying we would be home for midnight, because that came and went, so did one o'clock and two o'clock and still there was plenty of life in most of us. It was sheer happiness that kept us all going. It was a great success.

One person who came up to speak to me was a local man, who back in the forties had been a friend of my brother George. Something I had forgotten, but he reminded me, was that one bitterly cold day I had taken him into our cottage because he had short trousers on and his legs were red raw. I had rubbed vaseline on his legs and then sat him down in front of the fire and gave him a big thick slice of bread, butter and treacle and a cup of hot tea. He had always remembered me for that and now he was thanking me.

For me, the re-union was lovely in that we have made new friends and renewed old friendships. Clovelly will always hold a special place in my heart.

HARRY

After many months of organising, worry and writing, all the ex-evacuees that answered the 'call' came back to Clovelly. I had arranged with various families within the parish to provide bed and breakfast for two – three nights for most of those coming down, some had made their own arrangements with friends, a couple had brought their caravans down with them and it was all set for a wonderful week-end.

The weather was kind and everyone appeared happy, at least the dozen or more that crowded into our kitchen on the Friday evening. The barrel of beer was drastically lowered, as was my supply of wine, but there was so much to talk about, to laugh about and to look forward to.

The Saturday morning was booked to go to their old school at Wrinkleberry, to meet the headteacher, Tom Curtis, the Friends of Clovelly School and various parents and children. They all made the evacuees so very welcome, providing them with tea, coffee, biscuits and home-made cakes and each ex-evacuee was given a book, made by the children, as a keepsake of the re-union. All the while, the headteacher was moving about with a video recorder so that the meeting in the school could be recorded for posterity.

More photographs were taken in the playground and outside the gate and the one thing that impressed all the visitors, was the smallness of everything at the school. "How on earth did we all get into that tiny place." was the general comment.

That evening everyone seemed to enjoy the church service of thanksgiving and the presentation of the plaques, followed by the food, drinks, dancing and conversation in the Parish Memorial Hall.

One thing that came out of the re-union was a suggestion from one of the ex-evacuees, that the visitors should have a collection to form the start of a School Book Fund, to enable the headteacher to give an annual reward to children who had impressed him with their achievements. As the collection was being raised, several local people who had gone to school with evacuees in the war, and who now lived away from Clovelly, joined in and gave their contributions to the fund. In a matter of minutes nearly three hundred pounds had been raised and the intention is to top it up annually. There is now a Clovelly Evacuees School Book Fund and in July 1991, the first presentations were made.

Before departing to travel back to their homes, most of the visitors wanted to know when the next re-union would be held. The reply they received was, that it could be held whenever the majority wanted it, as long as someone else did the organising

If the re-union achieved nothing more, it brought old forgotten friends together and showed the people of Clovelly that in 1990 the evacuees are still grateful for what was done for them in 1940.

JEANIE

My impressions of the re-union was that it was very emotional, very electric and something that could not be repeated with the same atmosphere and feeling.

It was a beautiful weekend, one that you did not want to end. The weather was lovely, friendship oozed everywhere. It all went too fast.

RAY WILLS

Harry Clement, who I had known as a London evacuee at Clovelly in the war, who had been tall, slim with ginger hair, and who used to wear corduroy trousers, hob-nailed boots and a woollen jumper, wrote to me in 1990 to tell me about a re-union of ex-evacuees that he was trying to arrange; it would be Clovelly and was I interested. I agreed by return of post.

My wife and I drove down to Clovelly from Bristol on the Saturday morning and we stayed with Mrs Westlake, who had been my foster mother in the war. She was now elderly but was pleased to see us. We did not have to be introduced as we had been visiting her nearly every year for some time and she was to be my guest at the re-union party.

On the Saturday evening the church was packed for the thanksgiving service and the presentation of a plaque to the people of Clovelly, which would be fixed on the wall of the church. The party in the parish hall afterwards was amazing, with an abundance of food and wine with the food being served by the ladies of the Women's Institute to all the ex-evacuees and a group of elderly men and women who were the last survivors of all those who had taken children in during the war.

There were many other guests, as every visitor had invited some along, some were elderly, some were ex-school friends. The eating, drinking and talking went on for ages and there was background music of war-time songs of Vera Lynn and others.

Dancing started and went on to very late with everyone thoroughly enjoying themselves. The next day, most of us had to travel back home, hoping that there would be another re-union in the not too distant future.

RAY LAMB

What a re-union! Every emotion you could name and with so much friendship. It was as if we had never left Clovelly. People were fifty years older, some grey hair, some with no hair, middle age showing in the build of many of those present. But this did not detract from the welcome extended to everyone. If a face did not immediately bring a name to mind, the name tag that everyone wore, helped a lot and saved much embarrassment.

It seemed very strange going back to the school again, it appeared so small and makes me wonder where on earth did Mr Hesketh put us all in 1940. The staff, parents and children did us proud with the reception and the gifts. It was so good to look around the two little classrooms and the hall after all this time.

The stories that we swapped as we renewed friendships could have lasted longer than the time allotted. In all my life I have never felt so much warmth and love that stemmed from everyone. It was a collective feeling. If we had been a family of evacuees back in the early 1940's, then that family were back together again now.

The church service was great. It was packed and with the singing, I thought the roof was going to come off. I felt so at home in the church, I even went and had a look at where I used to sit to pump the organ. The old hand bellows are gone with the organ now converted to electric power.

At the party afterwards, with so many people to meet, to hug, to kiss and to greet. I laughed and I cried with so many of them, it was a wonderful feeling. Photographs were being handed around with comments such as, "Look at you then, that's when you were learning to swim", or "Was that the day we went blackberrying?" All the memories came flooding back. One lady showed me an autograph book that I had written in and signed on the 14 July 1941.

The whole weekend was so well organised that everything went smoothly. The food, drinks and the greetings were all well received with so many people to thank, but must we all wait another fifty years before we have another. There is so much more but my memory of small details is becoming dim and I am not sixty yet.

JILL

The weekend of 12/14 October was so lovely, I had to keep pinching myself to know that I was really back in Clovelly again, among the same people who were there with me 50 years previously.

How grateful I am to Eileen King for telling me about the re-union – what a wonderful occasion it was, thanks Harry.

All this only happened for me because in 1982, the family were on holiday in North Devon and I returned to the 'Retreat' for the first time since leaving Clovelly after the war. I then looked up Olive Brown (nee Jennings) and she found Eileen King for me.

In 1983, Joan and Johnny Searles celebrated their ruby wedding anniversary and the three bridesmaids, Pat, Jeanie and myself, met up again and that was a wonderful re-union. Then in 1990 to meet up with them and many others again was so terrific in an atmosphere of happiness. What happy memories. We were the lucky ones.

Where are they now?

Rose married John Brown and they live in Bexley, Kent.

Eileen married George King and they live in Bideford, Devon.

Jill married John Freeman and they live in East Grinstead, West Sussex.

Ray Lamb, a time-serving soldier, lived with his wife Mary in Erith, Kent, until his early death in January 1995.

Dene married Harry Rice and they still live in Peckham, London.

Georgina married Len Cook, a farmer of Fobbing, Essex.

Raymond Wills maried Dorothy and they live in Bishopsworth, Bristol.

Peter Scutts lives with his wife Joan in Broadstairs, Kent.

Jeanie married Peter Hanmer and they live in Clovelly, Devon.

The last contributor wishes to remain anonymous.

The author

Harry Clement enlisted in the Grenadier Guards at the age of 17, served for nearly six years and left in the rank of Gold Sergeant. He joined the Metropolitan Police in 1955 and was a career detective, serving mainly at New Scotland Yard in the Flying Squad and the national Regional Crime Squad: this work took him to many countries of the world investigating major crimes. In 1966 he was awarded the British Empire Medal for gallantry. He completed his police service in the rank of Detective Chief Superintendent, and is now retired to Clovelly. He is married to Pat and they have three adult children. His main interests are historical research, writing, and studying for a degree.